THE ACHILLES EFFECT

THE ACHILLES EFFECT

What Pop Culture is Teaching Young Boys about Masculinity

CRYSTAL SMITH

iUniverse, Inc.
Bloomington

The Achilles Effect
What Pop Culture is Teaching Young Boys about Masculinity

iUniverse books may be ordered through booksellers or by contacting:

iUniverse
1663 Liberty Drive
Bloomington, IN 47403
www.iuniverse.com
1-800-Authors (1-800-288-4677)

ISBN: 978-1-4502-8499-8 (sc)
ISBN: 978-1-4502-8501-8 (dj)
ISBN: 978-1-4502-8500-1 (ebk)

Printed in the United States of America

iUniverse rev. date: 01/28/2011

For Nikolas and Eliot

Table of Contents

Preface

The "woman's seat." That is the name my son assigned to the passenger seat of our car when he was just three years old. It was around the same time that I, as a female, was also denied the chance to drive our imaginary delivery truck or wear a hard hat on our make-believe construction site.

I was not exactly surprised to see this nascent gender bias in my son. It is exceedingly hard to avoid, not that I didn't try.

Knowing that popular culture is the source of many a child's ideas about gender, I limited my son's access to television and film. I considered gender balance in every toy purchase and I used gender-neutral language around him. Still, I knew that, despite my valiant efforts, my son would one day be exposed to the notion that certain behaviours are more appropriate for boys than girls—an idea that is far too pervasive and deeply entrenched in our society for me to block completely.

And there it was, arriving earlier than I ever would have guessed and manifested in arbitrary rules about who could sit where in a car.

Where this idea had come from—other children, teachers, books— was immaterial. The seed had been planted and I had to prevent it from taking root.

I began looking for information about the role of popular culture on a young boy's understanding of gender and, more specifically, masculinity, but found very little.

For young girls, the opposite is true. There are books, magazine articles, and blogs devoted to the impact of Disney princesses, Barbie, and other fictional females on little girls. There is also discussion about the lack of female characters in children's films and the sexualization of young girls. (The latter topic is addressed in a book called *The Lolita Effect*, which inspired the name of my book.)

Given the wealth of materials about young girls, pop culture, and gender, the near absence of similar information about young boys baffled me. There is certainly no shortage of things to talk about.

Traditional views of masculinity, ancient in origin but perpetuated in today's pop culture, teach boys to equate manhood with dominance, physical strength, and a decided absence of vulnerability. Boys who do not fit this masculine ideal feel the pressure to conform, going to extremes to prove their masculinity, or the pain of exclusion, suffering taunts like "wimp" or "nerd."

The idea of dominance, one of the hallmarks of traditional masculinity, also affects boys' views of femininity. By regularly characterizing males as the dominant sex, children's popular culture places females in a position of relative inferiority and teaches boys to devalue girls, women, and femininity in general.

Traditional masculinity is sustained in popular culture by gender stereotypes that affect boys as much as girls—a fact that is often overlooked. Boys looking to see themselves reflected in popular culture are instead faced with stereotyped views of what they should be, and introduced to many unhealthy ideas about males: boys don't cry; boys don't wear pink; boys don't play with dolls; boys are undisciplined, aggressive, noisy, and like to fight.

The Achilles Effect discusses the pop culture inputs that contribute to a young boy's understanding of masculinity and femininity. In the pages that follow, I combine recent research with examples from current children's movies, TV shows, books, and toy advertising to demonstrate what school-age boys are learning from the culture that surrounds them and how those lessons are affecting them. The programs and books I have chosen may lose currency, but they provide excellent examples of what parents can look for when evaluating gender portrayals in newer films, television programs, books, and toy advertisements.

The Achilles Effect is not about eliminating all aspects of traditional masculinity, but about broadening the term to be more inclusive of boys who do not fit the narrow definition we currently have. Nor is it about denying the differences between boys and girls. Certainly, there are some and boys need to know that it is okay to view girls as different. They also need to know that *different* does not mean *less than*.

The Achilles Effect discusses the early school-age years, but provides gender lessons that can be applied throughout a boy's life. I chose this age group, roughly equivalent to the kindergarten and primary school grades, because it is during these years that boys start to ascribe meaning to the words *boy* and *girl*.

This is also a time when they are faced with an onslaught of influences that shape their understanding of those two words. In order for them to develop healthy ideas about both sexes, it is critical that these early influences be balanced and gender-positive. Unfortunately, the majority of these influences, while considered innocuous by most adult observers, are anything but. Gender bias is not universal in children's entertainment, but it is very common, and affects boys' opinions of women and men, fathers and mothers, heroes and heroines. Even boys who do not watch a lot of television or film may absorb biased ideas about gender through peers who are more conversant with pop culture themes.

In researching *The Achilles Effect*, I examined some of the most popular films, TV shows, and books aimed at a male or mixed audience. In other words, no princess stuff—not because boys can't enjoy such materials, but because most do not. I looked closely at the way masculinity and femininity are presented and found some truly troubling notions, all of which I will discuss in detail here.

My choice of materials was, admittedly, arbitrary, veering from proven hits to personal favourites. To determine popularity in animated entertainment, I considered everything from the number of merchandise tie-ins to frequency on the television schedule. For books, I looked at public library reading lists and bestseller lists from online retailers. I checked the Common Sense Media website for more ideas and also included some of the films, TV shows, and books preferred by my own sons.

I would like to make clear that I am not advising against watching the programs or reading the books I discuss here. I am suggesting that parents strive for balance, not make pop culture an all-or-nothing proposition for their sons. I am also recommending that parents and caregivers become aware of what their sons are watching and take the initiative to talk to them about gender portrayals. In Chapter 7, I provide suggestions and tips to help adults (parents, caregivers, and even educators) begin discussions with boys about the gender bias that is so prevalent in the entertainment they see.

Readers may question my conclusions and disagree with my assessment of boys' popular culture, and that is okay. My ultimate goal is not to dictate what is right and what is wrong in pop culture, but to encourage discussion about a vitally important issue that is rarely talked about—boys and their often skewed understanding of gender.

A Word About Preschool Entertainment

When I first began researching this book, I examined preschool and school-age entertainment. I had planned to discuss both, but changed course when I discovered a sharp divergence between the two. Unlike programming aimed at school-age boys, where males and male stereotypes dominate, preschool TV shows offer far more nuanced portrayals of males and plenty of positive female characters.

Good television shows abound for this age group: *Bob the Builder* with its gentle and caring protagonist, strong female co-lead, and mixture of male and female supporting characters; *Arthur* and *Franklin the Turtle*, which provide balanced male characters and exceptional portrayals of engaged and involved mothers and fathers; and *Go Diego Go* and *Dora the Explorer*, both of whose protagonists play against type—he as a sensitive nurturer of animals and she as an adventurous and smart female lead. In addition to Dora, *Ni Hao Kai-Lan* and *Olivia* are other female-led shows that attract both male and female viewers.

Preschool programs clearly demonstrate that the key to achieving gender balance while appealing to a diverse audience is to create programs about kids in general, not about stereotyped versions of them—a lesson that seems to have been lost on the producers of programs for older children.

If preschool programs and the books associated with them can provide young boys with a balanced view of the world, why the abrupt change in tone when the target age group is older? I do not have the answer to that question, but as we will see in subsequent chapters, producers of school-age entertainment clearly could learn a lot from Diego, Dora, and Bob.

A Word of Thanks

My first book. What made me think I could actually pull this thing together? I knew I had the requisite research skills, honed through my BA in history and master's degree in library and information science. I have many years of experience volunteering with women's groups, including the Halton Women's Centre and The Pixel Project, which inspired me to add my voice to the many others already seeking greater gender balance in our world. I have been writing professionally for years and I take every chance I get to share my opinions on my *Achilles Effect* blog. But the support of some very important people is what really made this book possible.

I owe the men in my life a debt of gratitude for allowing me to escape into my "office" on countless evenings and weekends to work, even when it seemed, because I spent so much time watching TV and reading, that I wasn't really working at all. More specifically, I want to thank Karl for his endless patience and support and for being, in our sons' words, the best daddy ever. I also want to thank Nikolas and Eliot for inspiring me every day with their curiosity and creativity. (Additional thanks to Nikolas for being my movie buddy.)

A special word of thanks to my mother, Marilyn Papple, for instilling in me a sense of confidence and a belief that I could be anything I wanted to be, and for never telling me that collecting caterpillars, playing with Hot Wheels, and watching hockey were things that boys did.

Thanks to my sister, Chantal Smith, and other family members and friends— Grandma Dorothy Papple, Dad & Sarah, Michelle Walsh, Melvina Walter, and others too numerous to name here—who greeted news that I was writing my first book with encouragement and enthusiasm.

I also want to thank my crack team of editors and reviewers, Ginny Fanthome, Brenda Coonan, and Mackenzie Smith. I had no idea when I started working on this book just how easily I would lose perspective and fail to see where changes were needed. These three fabulous women generously gave their time to help me improve the final product. Thanks also to Laura Brooks for her expert advice on copy editing.

Lastly, a word of thanks to the wonderful people I have connected with through Twitter and my blog—Melissa Wardy from *Pigtail Pals*, Sharon Haywood from *Adios Barbie*, Amy Jussel from *Shaping Youth*, Erin McNeill from *Marketing, Media and Childhood*, and many others—who let me know that there is an audience eager for this book.

Introduction: Boys Will Be Boys

Boys will be boys. It's a loaded phrase and one that I hear frequently in the schoolyard, at birthday parties, at baseball practice—anywhere that young boys get together to socialize or play. My disdain for this phrase inspired me, in part, to write this book.

There is a lot to dislike about this expression. It carries with it a sense of inevitability, inferring as it does that boys are innately inclined toward stereotypically masculine behaviour—that nature trumps nurture, so to speak. It offers an excuse for the negative behaviours that are assumed to characterize boyhood—fighting, yelling, pushing, and shoving—while implying that aggression, rowdiness, and competitiveness are the truest signifiers of masculinity.

The phrase "boys will be boys" also draws a proverbial line in the sand, with boys on one side and girls on the other. Yes, girls and boys interact and play together and some may become good friends. But by the time they enter school, kids have learned that boys and girls are fundamentally different and that the behaviour that is accepted in one group is not okay for the other. From choices about toys and clothes to their reactions to stress, children understand early on that there are certain expectations attached to their sex.

For boys, those expectations are based on a very restrictive view of masculinity, defined by psychologist Ronald F. Levant as including: "the requirement to avoid all things feminine; the injunction to restrict one's emotional life; the emphasis on achieving status above all else; the injunction to be completely self-reliant; [and] the emphasis on toughness and aggression..."[1]

The impact of this view of masculinity can be seen at a very young age in boys who are embarrassed to show affection, reluctant to admit they are scared, or ashamed to cry when hurt. As boys get older, stereotyped behaviours become further entrenched, as any observer of a schoolyard can tell you. Watching kids interact on the playground, it is not unusual to see boys using intimidating language and postures to show toughness and dominance.

The situation does not improve for grown men. The emotional restraint they were taught as children often carries into adulthood, leaving them few outlets for their stress. Men feel consistent pressure to take on the role of provider. They are socialized to see their careers as the most important aspect of their lives and taught to believe that full-time employment is a sign of "successful masculinity"—a belief that many women share. Those who do not conform to the stereotype of the male breadwinner can experience a drop in self-esteem and a feeling that they have failed to become "real men."[2]

Fathers who do not work, whether by choice or not, face another level of disapproval. In a 2005 study conducted by Yale University, stay-at-home fathers were ranked the worst parents in comparison to employed fathers, employed mothers, and stay-at-home moms. The study also notes that fathers who stay home with their kids are viewed with disdain by employers, who assume that these men are incapable of finding work.[3] And in an Australian study, friends of male primary caregivers reported feeling disappointed in their friends for choosing to become full-time fathers.

Increasingly, the precepts of traditional masculinity are also thought to have an impact on men's physical health. Because concern for health is often seen as a feminine trait, many men are reluctant to visit the doctor or even ask questions when they are in their physician's office. Lifestyle is another issue. Generally speaking, men engage in more health-damaging behaviours than women—higher alcohol consumption, more risky behaviour, less healthy diet, less interest in maintaining a healthy weight— in part because such behaviours signify manliness. [4]

Traditional masculinity, as described by Levant, has deep roots. Family therapist Olga Silverstein and writer Beth Rashbaum note in *The Courage to Raise Good Men* that this narrow view of manhood has been with us since ancient times, first appearing in the stories of mythical heroes like Hercules, Jason, and Achilles.[5]

As implied by the title, the story of Achilles has particular relevance to the subject of this book. This legendary warrior epitomized the hyper-masculine ideal that we encounter to this day in popular culture and our wider society: he was physically strong, angry, vengeful, and sometimes disdainful of the feminine influences in his life.

Achilles was born of a mortal man and the goddess Thetis. A prophecy stated that Achilles would have either a long, dull life or a short, glorious life. Believing in the latter, his mother went to great lengths to protect him.

The story with which most of us are familiar involves Thetis dipping Achilles into the River Styx in an effort to make him immortal. The heel where she held him was not submerged and it became his sole physical vulnerability. In another variation on this story, Thetis attempted to burn away Achilles' mortality by searing him with fire.[6] Both versions of the story end with Thetis disappearing from her son's life and Achilles' father sending his infant son away to be educated by Chiron, a wise centaur who also mentored Hercules and Jason.

Training in the manly life of the warrior began immediately. Chiron toughened up the infant Achilles by feeding him the entrails and bowels of animals. By the age of twelve, he had Achilles outrunning horses and standing steadfast in coursing rivers for hours at a time.[7]

With the Trojan War raging, Chiron worked to prepare Achilles for life as a soldier, but Thetis interceded to prevent her son from joining the war. She dressed Achilles as a girl and hid him on the island of Scyros. (He was initially reluctant but acquiesced when he saw the beautiful girls he would be living with.)

Suspecting that Achilles was hidden on Scyros, the warrior Ulysses arrived on the island and promptly prepared a trap to identify him. He presented several gifts for the maidens, among which were a shield and spear. Achilles could not resist. As he grabbed the weapons and removed his feminine clothes, he was transformed from disguised maiden into supreme warrior, "mighty of limb" and surpassing Ulysses in size "by head and shoulders."[8]

When the time came to depart for the war, Achilles felt compassion and some sadness toward his new bride (a young woman he had impregnated when he forced himself on her), but he was motivated by a speech from Ulysses that appealed to his basest masculinity. In this speech Ulysses noted how Achilles was "profaned" by feminine dress and denied his chance to fulfill his destiny as a great warrior, an assessment with which Achilles heartily agreed.[9]

Achilles' skills as a soldier are documented in *The Iliad*, as are his nasty temper and bloodlust. In the book's opening scene, Achilles quarrels with Agamemnon over a battle prize and comes close to killing him. With his pride wounded, Achilles decides to drop out of the war and nurse his anger. He later returns to avenge the death of his close friend Patroclus. Achilles is greatly pained over the death of Patroclus, who was mistaken for Achilles on the battlefield, and his response is one of unrelenting violence.

He rejoins the war with palpable rage and a thirst for vengeance. He is described as gnashing his teeth, with eyes gleaming like fire, and compared to a fierce lion, roaring with fury—a man so frightening that the Trojans trembled at the sight of him.[10] In short, he was the ultimate warrior: motivated by anger, striking fear in the hearts of his enemies, and prepared to dominate and defeat anyone who crossed his path.

While the unbridled fury in *The Iliad* is not mirrored in the stories that school-age children hear and watch today, there are similar themes. Male protagonists are often cast as warriors. Like Achilles, they are ready to fight when slighted. They show little empathy for their enemies and are often portrayed as aggressive and violent, whether they are the hero or the villain.

The parallels between Achilles and today's animated men and boys do not end with their shared tendency toward violence. Like Achilles, some of the most popular characters, both warriors and others, are separated from their families and raised by male mentors. This separation breaks the bond between father and son but also serves the more important purpose of distancing a boy from the feminine influence of his mother.

The warrior ethos seen in Achilles' story and repeated in many of today's cartoons and books creates a stereotype that affects boys' ideas about manhood, perpetuating the form of traditional masculinity described by Levant, teaching boys to distinguish behaviour that is manly from behaviour that is not, and making it clear that acting girly is wrong.

Along with the warrior, the other male stereotype that dominates children's popular culture is his diametric opposite—the so-called nerd. As sociologist Ellen Jordan notes in her 1995 article "Fighting Boys and Fantasy Play: the construction of masculinity in the early years," which appeared in the journal *Gender and Education*, these two types have tremendous influence over a boy's ideas about masculinity, his overall gender identity, and his view of femininity.

According to Jordan, the "warrior discourse" (which comes from the mass media) is the source of most boys' understanding of masculinity. This discourse offers two extremes of masculinity. In the first position are the warriors, heroes, or leaders. The warriors' masculinity is unquestioned and framed by the less manly behaviour of the subordinate group—the wimps and nerds.

Because they do not fit the warrior ideal, the weaker boys create their own version of masculinity, defining the term as "not female." Using this alternative definition of masculinity enables them to "redress insecurities and ambivalences about their ability to be male." In other words, the less traditionally masculine boys prove their manhood by ensuring that they never act like girls.

The male/female dualism that results from the warrior discourse is, according to Jordan, so deeply entrenched that non-sexist approaches to child rearing cannot eradicate it. As she states in her conclusion, there are two constraints within which parents concerned about gender equity need to operate: "children's early adoption of a firmly established gender identity, and the power of the 'warrior discourse' of masculinity to grip the imaginations of little boys looking for guidance on how their gender identity is to be manifested in their behaviour and beliefs."

Her solution? A broader gender identity for both boys and girls. Parents need to convey to children:

that gender identity does not necessarily involve either a monopoly over certain activities nor a rejection of others; that there are a number of valid ways of being male and of being female; that overlap in activities does not deny gender identity to either group; that activities are to be evaluated by whether they are good or bad in human terms, not by their gender appropriateness.[11]

The female identity has already been expanded to some extent. While girls are inundated with images of extreme femininity (thank you Barbie and Disney), they are also applauded for breaking out of the little pink box that TV producers, toy marketers, and even some caregivers would confine them to. For boys the situation is quite different—venturing beyond the borders of manly behavior is usually not encouraged and may be actively discouraged.

The contrast between the experiences of each sex is striking. Girls who excel at physics and math are lauded. Boys who get an A in home economics, not so much. Girls can play hockey, but boys cannot take ballet. Girls can like Bakugan, but boys cannot like Barbie. Girls can play with Hot Wheels, but boys cannot play with a dollhouse.

By changing conventional wisdom about what it means to be male, as Jordan suggests, we can give boys the freedom to pursue interests without regard for their gender appropriateness—a freedom that girls currently enjoy—and combat the destructive notion that certain behaviours are inherently unmanly.

Challenging traditional ideas about masculinity will also help in the fight for sexual equality. The devaluing of girls and all things feminine—a major imperative of both the warrior discourse and Levant's definition of masculinity—perpetuates the idea that males are the stronger sex and that females are inherently weaker and inferior. By changing the way we see masculinity, we can soften the arbitrary line that divides masculine behaviours from feminine. These behaviours will then cease to be positioned as opposites and start to be seen, in Jordan's words, in human terms with no gender assigned. Boys will then come to understand that males and females, while different in some ways, are equal in every way.

Before I am accused of trying to turn boys soft or make them into "honorary women,"[12] let me state that a wider view of masculinity does not mean denying a boy's inclination for typically masculine activities and toys—boys who love trucks and motorcycles should be allowed to play with trucks and motorcycles.

At the same time, boys should be given the opportunity to follow other interests, even if those interests lead them into territory traditionally considered to be feminine. A boy who plays with loud construction vehicles one day may very well choose to play with a baby doll the next day. Under a broader definition of masculinity, we would no longer believe that this behaviour is a sign of weakness, but begin to accept that a boy's natural instincts to learn and experience new things will lead him in many different directions.

Expanding the definition of masculinity from its current, narrow form requires us to address one of the main sources of gender bias in a boy's life—popular culture and the stereotypes within it.

A boy's socialization into particular gender roles actually begins in infancy, with caregivers being the primary influence. As they reach the age of about five or six—the age range I am discussing here—boys become active in developing their own gender identity and begin looking for new role models to emulate.[13] Very often, boys this age look to TV shows and movies for these role models—places where gender stereotypes are the rule and not the exception.

In fact, stereotypes are so ingrained in children's media and the wider culture that they go virtually unnoticed. They are absorbed by children gradually and almost by osmosis, a fact noted by Cardiff University journalism professor Justin Lewis in a 2001 documentary about Disney's influence on children:

> I think it's a mistake for us to imagine that the only way that media affect us is through an immediate impact on the way we think. The way media influences the way we think is much less immediate and much less a sort of straight forward impact ... [it] is much more a question of creating a certain environment of images that we grow up in and that we become used to and after a while those images will begin to shape what we know and what we understand about the world. And that's not an immediate wiz-bang effect. That's a slow and accumulative effect and much more subtle.[14]

It would be an oversimplification to say that the media is entirely to blame for children's skewed views of gender, but there is no denying the impact of television and film. In 2001, in the *Encyclopedia of Women and Gender*, psychology professors L. Monique Ward and Allison Caruthers summarized the findings of some 76 different studies into the impact of media on children's perceptions of gender. They began by describing how difficult it is to assess the effect of media because of the many variations in the ways people interact with media: repeated exposure versus one-time viewing; active versus passive viewing; and different responses to the genre, medium, format, and tone of the programming. The characteristics of the viewer and his or her perspective on gender can also have an effect on how media images are interpreted.

That being said, the researchers did find evidence—very strong in some cases—of media impact on a viewer's ideas about gender:

- Greater exposure to mainstream media gender portrayals, which tend to be traditional and stereotypical, increases support for sexist attitudes, especially toward women.
- Mainstream media portrayals also reinforce stereotyped notions of what each sex does and how they act, while strengthening a viewer's preferences for traditional occupations and activities.
- Conversely, exposure to non-traditional gender portrayals seems to encourage more flexible ideas about gender and gender roles.

The bottom line? Although more research is needed, the authors concluded that "frequent or directed exposure to stereotypical images appears to strengthen traditional orientations to gender, while frequent or directed exposure to egalitarian images appears to weaken them."[15]

Although very influential, television and film are not the only sources of biased attitudes towards women and men. Boys see gender stereotypes consistently across all types of entertainment, including books and toys, and in the language they encounter in their daily lives. When combined, these separate forces shape a boy's perception of masculinity and, by extension, femininity.

I liken it to a puzzle coming together. TV and film form one corner of the puzzle. Books form another, and toys another. Language and communication complete the outline. With each stereotyped image that a child sees, the puzzle is gradually pieced together until the picture, unbalanced as it may be, is complete.

The image that emerges would look rather like a pyramid, with the strong warrior males on top, the weaker boys on the bottom, and girls somewhere on the periphery—present, but not really part of the big picture.

The Achilles Effect will help us create a new picture for boys—one that frees them from the restraints imposed by traditional masculinity. It will examine the messages sent by popular culture and discuss strategies for countering those messages. And it will allow us to begin the process of redefining masculinity so we can offer our sons a whole new world of experiences and possibilities, and show them that boys can be so much more than just "boys."

Chapter 1: Warriors, Wimps, Brats, and Clowns: The Impact of Male Stereotypes on Boys

$$\sim\!\!\sim$$

I remember my first encounter with gender stereotypes in children's cartoons. The opening scene of an episode of *What's New Scooby-Doo* showed two boys looking up at a large roller coaster. When one expressed his fear of the ride, the other said to him with disgust, "Don't be a girl."

The character's words hit me like a slap. Having previously limited my son's television viewing to the kind and gentle *Bob the Builder* and the educational *Mighty Machines*, I was quite unprepared for this abrupt change in tone. Despite my shock, I maintained my composure, calmly told my son that this program was inappropriate for him, then found something else for him to watch. (Sadly, television had become something of a necessity for my older son since the birth of my younger one, who was rather feisty and difficult to settle at nap time.)

At that time I was not researching or even considering writing a book, which is why I lack a proper citation for the episode, but that scene was an eye-opener for me. I had always thought that gender stereotypes affected only girls and women. With that one sentence, I realized that boys could suffer just as much as girls from the harsh, gender-based judgments of others.

The roller coaster scene became something of a catalyst for me. I began to look more closely at depictions of boys and men in children's popular culture and I discovered that kids' films, television, and books are rife with stereotyped male characters. These characters sustain and reinforce the brand of masculinity that first emerged in ancient hero stories and prevails still—one that assigns value to boys according to their level of manliness. Warriors, being the most stereotypically masculine, are considered the ideal, while more effeminate or soft boys are relegated to the bottom of the heap. These male types are juxtaposed against females, who, presumed to be inherently weaker, provide a baseline of feminine behaviour against which all males are measured.

As will be shown in subsequent chapters, gender stereotypes cast a wide net, affecting portrayals of fathers, mothers, and heroes in pop culture. But they also have an impact on the everyday perceptions boys have of themselves and the women and girls in their lives.

Snips and Snails and Puppy Dog Tails: That's What Boys are Made Of

While writing this book, that old rhyme from my childhood kept coming to mind. And while male characters are not necessarily portrayed as yucky—at least not in the TV shows and films aimed at school-age boys—they tend to come in rather one-dimensional packaging.

Male characters in children's popular culture are arranged in a hierarchy similar to that seen among pack animals like wolves and other dogs: alphas at the top, omegas at the bottom, and betas somewhere in between. In kids' pop culture, the warrior is the alpha, the wimp[1] is the omega, and the bully, clown, and brat characters are betas, albeit closer to the bottom than the top. This hierarchy is not new, but the fact that it still exists, despite changes in gender roles in society, is not encouraging.

These characterizations of males may seem insignificant but they are not. As McGill University's Paul Nathanson and Katherine K. Young state in their 2001 book *Spreading Misandry*, "there is nothing trivial about pop culture. It is the folklore, the conventional wisdom, of an urban, industrial society...Almost all sitcoms—let alone crime shows, soap operas and 'dramedies'—have what are often called 'relevant' plots and subplots, episodes that teach moral or political lessons of some kind."[2]

Nathanson's and Young's comments, made in reference to entertainment for the teen and adult age groups, apply equally to children's entertainment. Lessons of a sort abound in kids' TV and film, and for boys they are not entirely positive. By placing boys in distinct categories and implying that the most stereotypically masculine boys have the most worth, pop culture teaches boys to value traditionally masculine traits, like aggression, over any other characteristics boys might possess.

The warrior (or alpha male) is the most prevalent of the male stereotypes in film and television programming aimed at boys. Superheroes are the most recognizable warrior characters and I will discuss them in detail in a later chapter. Even without them, there are plenty of examples of the warrior—a male character who is defined by stoicism, a quick temper, and a touch of rebelliousness. He usually tries to do the right thing, but often employs violence to overcome challenges and solve problems. He is easy to spot, given his less-than-sunny disposition, his air of toughness, and his independent streak.

Dan from the television series *Bakugan Battle Brawlers* is one. (The show features a group of tween-aged children who engage mythical creatures called Bakugan in battles for supremacy over the forces of evil.) Dan, as described on the show's website, is a leader who is quick to temper, ambitious, and "more street smart than book smart."[3] In other words, Dan is a poster child for stereotypical alpha male behaviour. Dan's appearance underscores the kind of boy he is. Sunglasses rest on top of his head of tousled brown hair. He wears fingerless gloves and a red and black outfit that is equal parts athletic and "street"—a look that suggests action and competitiveness. His speech is peppered with tough talk like "You're going down!"

Shun, another Bakugan brawler, is the stereotypical strong, silent type. His purple and black outfit and ponytailed hair suggest martial arts, a look befitting a loner who approaches the Bakugan game "like a Ninja warrior."[4] As a supposedly more cerebral fighter, Shun is withdrawn and taciturn, unlike the more hotheaded Dan.

As can be assumed from its title, the TV series *Power Rangers: RPM* has its share of warrior characters as well. Scott, the red Power Ranger, was in the military and seems to be weighed down by a great deal of anger and resentment. Scott has a difficult relationship with his father, which stems from his father's inability to accept and value his son for the man he is. To prove that he is tough and capable, Scott adopts all the hallmarks of the warrior—simmering anger, short temper, and machismo.

Scott frequently butts heads with Dillon, the other warrior in the show. In contrast to military man Scott, Dillon is the loner rebel. Dressed in black leather, gunning it through the desert in his muscle car, Dillon is the wild one who resists being tamed by the rules of the Power Rangers. Eventually he joins the group, but he maintains his reputation as a bit of a loose cannon.

Some programs offer a slightly more progressive take on the warrior. Ben Tennyson of *Ben 10: Alien Force* is one of the few male leads who comes across as a balanced character. He has a gentler disposition than his counterparts in other action shows and is referred to by his female cousin as sensitive and well-mannered. He gets along well with her and with other girls without appearing soft or overly feminized.

Anakin Skywalker of the film *Star Wars: The Clone Wars* is another nice-guy warrior. While aggressive in battle and very serious about his role as a Jedi warrior, Anakin, like Ben Tennyson, is a decent young man. He treats others with respect, including his young female apprentice, Ahsoka. He admits when he makes mistakes and he trusts Ahsoka to share in the decision making instead of doing all of the heavy lifting himself.

In the television show based on the *Clone Wars* film, Anakin becomes a little more stereotypical, appearing to be more of a risk-taker and occasionally more domineering over Ahsoka. The TV program also conveys the true nature of the warrior when Anakin's mentor, Obi-Wan Kenobi, warns Anakin that emotional attachments are risky for a Jedi. (It turns out that he is speaking from experience, as he was once in love with Duchess Satine Karyne.[5]) This statement makes clear that no matter how kind the Jedi may be—and Obi-Wan and Anakin both seem to be generous in nature—they are warriors first. As such, they must not allow emotion to get in the way of their battle against evil.

Of course, control of emotion has been an essential part of warrior training for centuries. The legendary Spartans of ancient Greece reportedly whipped boys as young as seven and forced them to sleep naked in the winter so they would learn to endure pain and hardship without complaint.[6] (Achilles was similarly trained by his mentor.)

In 1521, Niccolo Machiavelli wrote in *The Art of War* that virtuous leadership comes from emotional self-discipline—a military leader must know his limitations and act rationally at all times. Similar self-discipline is required in the commander's subordinates who must follow a hierarchical chain of command and accept their place in that hierarchy without objection.[7] Machiavelli and the military leaders who followed him also believed that in order to work effectively together as a group, soldiers required rigid discipline. There was no room to consider the concerns or needs of individuals within the unit.

Because strong emotional reactions to a tense situation can affect a soldier's ability to make decisions, military training has exploited soldiers' emotions in other ways. To ensure that a soldier's conviction does not waver, military leaders have used techniques like creating a sense of overwhelming pride or patriotism[8] and cultivating a fear or hatred of the enemy to inspire troops. (The latter is also a Machiavellian idea.)[9]

Modern military leaders are beginning to take a different view of emotional issues, at least in some parts of the world. Having seen the impact of ignoring or manipulating the emotions of its troops, the US Army has recently introduced Army Master Resilience Training, which aims to help soldiers avoid troubles like post-traumatic stress. The program "focuses on the five dimensions of strength: emotional, social, spiritual, family, and physical."[10] That the army has acknowledged a need for such training underscores the importance of addressing emotional troubles among soldiers and proves that a strong warrior capable of vanquishing the enemy can still be emotionally open.

The combat role, manifested in children's cartoons as a fight between good and evil, gives rise to what is, perhaps, the most troublesome aspect of the warrior ethos in children's popular culture—the tendency to respond aggressively when threatened or provoked. All warrior characters, even the gentler ones, frequently and willingly participate in intensely violent battles against their enemies.

Some TV producers attempt to couch the violence by having their main characters fight by proxy. In *Bakugan Battle Brawlers*, Dan, Shun, and the others call upon mythical creatures known as Bakugan to lead the fight against the dark forces they face. Similarly, the human characters in the cartoon series *Chaotic* and *Pokemon* use non-humans to wage their battles. *Ben 10: Alien Force* sees the character of Ben transform himself into any one of ten alien superheroes, making it appear less like he is directly involved in the fighting. Other programs do not spare the humans: the Power Rangers, the *Hot Wheels Battle Force 5* team, and the Jedi all fight directly, using various high-tech vehicles and weapons.

Whether they are involved directly or peripherally, the protracted and often graphic fight scenes involving these characters make aggression and a desire for dominance appear to be essential or even praiseworthy male traits.

The pro-violence message sent to boys through these programs is also communicated through popular toys and the marketing that surrounds them.

Advertising for toys like Hot Wheels and Matchbox cars, Transformers, and Nerf guns all emphasize aggression and competition. Even toys that were once gender-neutral, like Lego, have gotten into the game. The Lego website shows a stark gender divide, with many of the so-called boys' toys being designed to vanquish some kind of enemy. Their Bionicles line, aimed at eight-year-olds but played with by children younger than the recommended age, is particularly disconcerting. Among the main characters are the Skrall, who are described as follows on the site:

> arrogant, vicious, brutal, fear nothing and care about even less. They are just waiting for the opportunity to start taking whatever they want, whenever they want it. They are incredibly skilled fighters, with or without weapons. What they may lack in technique they make up for with sheer bludgeoning power and strength.[11]

While not a word one might expect to see in a description of a toy, *bludgeoning* is just one of many violent terms used in the advertising for boys' toys. Others on this list include: arsenal, battle, blast, dangerous, deadly, fierce, firepower, force, hothead, power, savage, scorching, and, of course, warrior. The use of martial language, also common in sports broadcasts, is intentional and serves to underscore the commonly held notion that boys should be tough, defiant, and always ready to fight.

Violent messages and images also appear in the clothing marketed to boys. Parents browsing the racks at their local department store might be surprised to find among the toddler clothes a T-shirt with a Transformer-like robot shooting orange lasers from its eyes. Skulls are another common motif, appearing in clothing for boys aged one to twelve at mainstream retailers like Zellers, The Children's Place, and H&M. To add to the overall effect, many of the designs look like they were spray painted and text is often written in a graffiti-styled font. Fashions like these dovetail perfectly with the messages delivered by toy advertising, telling boys that fighting and toughness are cool.

All of these influences—the hero characters that dominate children's movies and TV, the toys, the fashions, and the book series that are spun off from shows like *Clone Wars, Bakugan Battle Brawlers* and *Ben 10: Alien Force*—reinforce the warrior discourse that Ellen Jordan discussed in her 1995 study "Fighting Boys and Fantasy Play."

Jordan wrote that children become aware of the distinction between *boy* and *girl* as toddlers, but gender really begins to matter to them during the early school-age years. During this time they are "actively looking for guidance on what is gender-appropriate behaviour." Turning to pop culture, young boys come face-to-face with the image of the warrior, an idea that has a "powerful hold" on their imaginations and a strong influence on their perception of masculinity.[12]

This idea of masculinity, as defined by popular male characters like Dan and Anakin, tells boys that for men, anger is a legitimate response to being wronged and negotiation is not an option. It also introduces them to the idea that men should speak softly and carry a big stick— that is, spend less time discussing their feelings or frustrations and more time threatening and intimidating their "enemies."

As Jordan postulates in her study, any man who does not act the warrior part is positioned as his subordinate—the "weakling" or "coward."[13] Current popular culture serves up many characters to fill that role.

In the Bakugan universe, there is Marucho, who contrasts sharply with Dan and Shun in both character and appearance. Although he is only one year younger than the other two, he dresses in a childish blue and white sailor suit. In a later version of the show, subtitled *Gundalian Invaders*, he sports a new but still babyish outfit of short overalls. The other characters recognize and respect his brilliance, but because he is smart, he is depicted as less warrior-like than Dan or Shun: he wears glasses, has a high voice, and is significantly smaller than all of the other brawlers, including the females.

In the TV series *Hot Wheels Battle Force 5*, the character Spinner is noticeably smaller and less muscular than his hulking brother and the other team members, including female Agura. According to the team's sentient computer, Spinner possesses "unparalleled hacking abilities" which seems to imply that he is a computer geek.[14] He was recruited to provide tech support for the Battle Force team and does not drive his own vehicle—he rides with his brother, Sherman. Although Spinner is not the worst example of the wimp stereotype, the fact that he is physically smaller and the only character to express any trepidation about the team's various missions indicates that he is less "warrior" and more "weakling." (I should note that this show does win points for putting another spin on the so-called nerd character—Sherman is built like a linebacker but also extremely smart and not afraid to show it.)

Even Peter Parker, the alter-ego of Spider-Man, is considered a geek. He and his friends, Harry and Gwen, are collectively referred to as the "nerd herd" by the cheerleaders and jocks in their school.

The wimp character is also well represented in recent films. Flint, the skinny and brainy scientist from *Cloudy with a Chance of Meatballs*, saves the day but is noticeably less masculine than his fisherman father and the brawny police chief. It is even implied by his eventual love interest, Sam, that Flint is a nerd. Ash from *Fantastic Mr. Fox* lacks athletic prowess and is told he dresses "like a girl." And Arthur in *Shrek the Third* is cast as the stereotypical 98-pound weakling.

The nerd character makes an appearance in children's literature too. In the book *How to Train Your Dragon*, male lead Hiccup is described as useless, on the small side, with a face that is "almost entirely unmemorable."[15] He is ridiculed and considered feeble, especially in comparison to his father, Stoick the Vast.

In the first book of the *Zac Power* series, Zac's older brother is called "geeky" and described as scared and hopeless. Like Marucho, he is very smart and wears glasses. (He does prove helpful to Zac, but is notably less assertive and less confident than his brother.)

The character of Geronimo Stilton, in the eponymous children's book series, is the bookish and sensitive male editor of a big-city newspaper. Geronimo has many good qualities, like loyalty, intelligence, and compassion, but he is clearly positioned as a weakling.

The adventures Geronimo undertakes are rarely of his own choosing. He is often pushed or cajoled into his various expeditions, is scared of his own shadow, and very clumsy. He is frequently reduced to tears and his constant crying is depicted as ridiculous, not as a legitimate emotional response. He is teased by his cousin, harassed by his grandfather, and shown up regularly by his sister. While Geronimo ultimately resolves the problems he faces, the resolutions tend to emerge by accident and not before he is humiliated and often trod upon by others. There are lessons here about succeeding despite the odds, but Geronimo comes across predominantly as passive and meek—traits that make him an easy target for his stronger and more assertive friends and relatives.

Wimp characters like Geronimo, Flint, and Hiccup are, to some degree, archetypes—they face difficulties but ultimately triumph. Their stories contain obvious lessons, such as when Hiccup notes that he has to become a hero the hard way.[16] These characters also have some redeeming qualities, exemplified by Flint and Hiccup who, despite the negative feedback they receive from others, have the courage and confidence to follow their instincts—the former in devising wacky inventions, the latter in training instead of killing dragons.

For these reasons, some boys may relate to these characters and find common ground with them. But because "geek" narratives never show the strong males being frightened, getting picked on, or failing in a humiliating fashion, the overall message is a negative one. Nerd characters may be kind, decent, smart, and even victorious in the end, but they are still not positioned as equal to the stronger, tougher boys and will seldom be regarded as heroes in the traditional sense of the word. Want proof? Ask any young boy whether he would rather be Geronimo or Anakin—chances are pretty good he'll choose the latter.

Ranking above the nerd on the male hierarchy is his frequent nemesis—the bully. (Because they tend to be less virtuous than the warriors, bully characters do not rank as high as Dan, Shun, Anakin, and company.) Like their chosen victims, some bully characters are archetypes. They are so extremely nasty that their presence serves only one purpose—demonstrating how an irredeemably evil character will get his due. Some of the better examples of this character include Snotlout, the boy who harasses and picks on protagonist Hiccup in *How to Train Your Dragon*, and the grasshoppers from *A Bug's Life*, who treat the ants as slaves. As archetypes, characters like this are not nearly as problematic as the passive bullies that are seen in kids' pop culture.

The passive bully is not as overtly evil as the bad guy characters mentioned above, but he does employ bullying tactics in his attempts to dominate others. Fred from the *Time Warp Trio* series of books uses intimidating language to assert himself, as does Harry from *Horrible Harry* on occasion. Buford from the television program *Phineas and Ferb* also uses this kind of talk, especially in relation to the nerd character on the show, and Geronimo Stilton's grandfather regularly berates and belittles his grandson.

Since none of these characters are admonished for their behaviour and because they are all still welcomed into their peer group (or respected as elders in the family, in the case of Stilton), children may begin to see their posturing as a normal response for boys. By implying that insults and the language of aggression are typical or even expected in male-to-male interactions, the creators of these mildly bullying characters are, however subtly, indicating that competition and jockeying for position are essential elements of male relationships.

In their quest for dominance, these characters personify the "big wheel imperative" described by psychologist William Pollack in *Real Boys*, which dictates that men must always try to outdo each other and never settle for second place.[17] In this line of thinking, there is little room for understanding or sensitivity—manliness is equated with a continual game of one-upmanship. While some might argue that such portrayals are reflecting reality—that men are naturally inclined toward competition with one another—the inclusion of such characters in children's popular culture serves to glorify this kind of behaviour and reinforces the idea that bullying others is a sign of strength.

Somewhere between the bully and the nerd on the male hierarchy lies the clown. This character makes frequent appearances in kids' pop culture and is always male. Clown characters are not necessarily bad—they provide comic relief and are well-liked by the audience. Yet they are always depicted as less manly than the alpha-male characters: Ziggy on *Power Rangers: RPM* is noticeably more frail than the other males and also possesses a higher voice; Shaggy on the various *Scooby-Doo* series is skinnier and has a more slovenly appearance than the clean-cut, fit-looking Fred; Peyton from *Chaotic* talks like a California surfer dude and is less "handsome" than lead male Tom; and the constantly fretful C3-P0 in *Star Wars: The Clone Wars* is played as fussy and effeminate.

Last among male stereotypes is the brat. Unlike the clown, who tends to be goofy but not mean-spirited, the brat has a subversive streak. A character whose territory is most famously occupied by Bart Simpson of *The Simpsons*, the brat is always a boy. Although intended to be funny, brat characters frequently cause trouble at school, adding an anti-authority undercurrent to the already negative messages they deliver about boyhood. The two protagonists in the very popular *Captain Underpants* series of books are prime examples.

In this series the two lead males—George and Harold—are described as clever and good-hearted, yet they cause mischief at school. The excuse given? They are expected to "sit still and pay attention for *seven hours a day*" and neither of them is very good at that.[18] Or maybe it's that they suffer from "I.B.S.S. (Incredibly Boring School Syndrome)."[19] Regardless of the cause, these two play pranks and cause trouble for their teachers and fellow students. Because they never seem to learn from or show remorse for what they have done, Harold and

George send the message that bad behaviour is cool and school is not. Boys who struggle in school might identify with characters like Harold and George and be entertained by their antics, but they will not find positive ways to deal with the alienation they feel.

The anti-school message is reinforced in this series by the depictions of teachers. These characters are regularly ridiculed and given names like Mr. Fyde (mystified), Miss Anthrope (misanthrope), Mr. Meaner (misdemeanor), and Ms. Ribble (miserable). The latter is often referred to as "mean" and described as speaking harshly, snapping, and screaming at her students.[20] Through these unsympathetic portrayals of teachers, the books' author seems to making excuses for, or even justifying, the boys' pranks.

A similar anti-school message is delivered in at least one video game aimed at young children. In *Mario & Luigi: Bowser's Inside Story*, the character of Toad, presumed to be coming home from school early, notes that his teacher was going on and on, "blah, blah, blah." Instead of admonishing him, his mother calls him a "naughty scamp" and continues getting ready for dinner. A video game is not the place one would expect moral lessons, but images like this do promote the idea that school is a nuisance and something that does not need to be taken seriously.

Negativity towards school also seeps into some unexpected areas, like boys' clothing. In some stores, T-shirts stating that "before homework kills trees, it must be stopped" hang alongside the skulls and graffiti I mentioned earlier. Another shirt, seen at Canadian retailer Zellers, includes a message with key words struck out: "Mom, I'll do my homework right ~~away then~~ after I ~~finish I will~~ play my video games." (One can imagine that Harold and George would be proud to sport such fashions, which, for the record, are not available in the girls' department.)

Much has been made recently of boys' poor performance in school, their inability to pay attention, and their general disenchantment with the classroom. There are many reasons for this lack of interest in school and popular culture is not entirely to blame, but characters who disdain school and the rules within it contribute to a boy culture that tells young males that bratty behaviour is cool and doing well at school is nerdy.

Harry from the *Horrible Harry* series offers a different take on the brat character—he demonstrates that boys can be flawed but still have redeeming qualities. Harry is not a perfect child. He likes to play pranks, frequently taunts and teases his classmate Sidney, and regularly seeks revenge when he is slighted. Yet, unlike Harold and George, he is considerate and a good friend to the other children. He is smart and seems to enjoy school. He and his classmates show a genuine caring for one another, despite their occasional disagreements. Harry's stories showcase the kinds of challenges and personality conflicts that students his age face while demonstrating the consequences—both positive and negative—of the kids' actions and decisions. These are lessons that few other brat characters convey.

No matter how they are depicted—as strong, weak, goofy, or bratty—male characters are drawn together by a nearly complete absence from the domestic realm.

Much of the entertainment aimed at boys focuses on fighting or adventure and, as such, takes place outside of the home, but in stories where home life is depicted, domestic chores and child rearing are typically portrayed as the work of females.

Children's picture books are one example. Studies have shown that female characters in these books are 3 ½ times more likely to perform nurturing behaviours like child care. Twice as many male characters are shown working outside the home. Men also have a far wider range of careers to choose from, while women tend to be placed in jobs that emphasize nurturing and caring, like nurse, maid, and nanny.[21]

Toy advertising also reinforces the notion that males are less suited to domesticity than females. Looking at one major source of advertising—the glossy catalogues sent out by toy sellers in the pre-Christmas season—there is clear evidence of the intended audience for each toy. It is not just the pink colour-coded pages found in the catalogues of major retailers like Toys R Us that tell children who belongs with which toy—it is the images of who is playing with them. While toy kitchens seem to include children of both sexes most of the time, dollhouses are shown to be the exclusive domain of girls. Tea sets, baby dolls, carriages, shopping carts, and vacuums are also cast in a pink glow.

In contrast, boys are never shown playing with dolls or dollhouses. In fact, other than the kitchen, the closest they get to the home is the garage or the workshop—places in which girls, according to toy sellers, never set foot.

When considering the impact of this kind of advertising, it is important to remember that parents are as much a part of the target audience as children. Parents decide which toys to buy for their children and, through their purchase decisions, influence their children's understanding of the gender-appropriateness of toys.[22] Boys who are denied a baby doll, toy vacuum, or grocery cart receive clear lessons in what kind of play is acceptable for male children.

And what is the impact when a boy who wants to role-play by taking care of baby, cooking, or cleaning is admonished for seeking out this type of play? The effects can be far-reaching. A boy who is told that his chosen mode of play is wrong or "only for girls" will not soon forget it. He may become self-conscious or ashamed of his choice. He will miss out on valuable opportunities to explore and make sense of the world around him. He will also lose the chance to satisfy his natural curiosity about the things he encounters in everyday life, which, whether adults like it or not, include babies, strollers, brooms and mops, aprons, pots, pans, and other so-called mommy stuff.

His sense of what it means to be female will also be affected. When feminine activities and interests are dismissed as not worthy of boys, young males begin to learn that girls occupy a very different place in the world from boys.

If adult attitudes towards toys and play do not diminish a boy's opinion of femininity, pop culture portrayals of females very well could. In addition to being locked into domesticity by toy manufacturers, girls are portrayed, for the most part, in a demeaning and stereotypical manner in film and television, where their appearance and behaviour contrast sharply with that of their male counterparts.

Sexualization is one problem facing female characters. While sexualized images may not mean much to a six- or seven-year-old boy, they add to the "environment of images" described by Justin Lewis,[23] affecting boys' ideas about how girls should look and behave.

The girls on *Bakugan Battle Brawlers* and *Pokemon* are among the most highly sexualized. Although they are children, they have large breasts and long legs that are emphasized by their revealing clothes. The women in the film *Star Wars: The Clone Wars* do not fare much better. They are strong characters, but their strength is undermined by their clothing: the evil Ventress wears a cleavage-baring top; Ahsoka wears a tiny skirt that shows her legs; and Padmé Amidala sports a white catsuit that accentuates her breasts and posterior. The male counterparts of these women, it should be noted, are fully clothed in loose-fitting garments at all times. Female and male superheroes show similar discrepancies in clothing. The men are completely covered (although in form-fitting suits), while the females typically show more skin.

Regardless of how they are dressed, many female characters exhibit terribly stereotyped behaviour. The character of Karen on *SpongeBob SquarePants* is a particularly egregious example. She is a computer known as WIFE (Wired Integrated Female Electroencephalograph). That the role of wife could be filled by a machine is troubling enough, but this portrayal goes further. Karen is possessed of a whining voice and nasty demeanor. As she chastises her husband, he expresses regret at having installed "nagging software" in her. Eventually he turns her off completely.[24]

Emotions also tend to run higher in female characters than in males. In the video game *Mario & Sonic at the Summer Olympic Games,* female characters Peach, Daisy, and Amy compete at the same events as the males, but react quite differently when they lose. Their male competitors react with disappointment and even frustration, but never cry, while the females sob and even fall to the ground in tears.

Other excessively emotional girls include Pearl from *SpongeBob SquarePants*, who is pouty and selfish and, in at least one episode, uses tears to manipulate her father. Ms. Marvel from the animated series *Super Hero Squad* shrieks loudly at her male counterparts when they threaten the team's mode of conveyance, the HeliCarrier. She is even referred to sarcastically as "Mom" by Iron Man.[25] But few can top Candace from *Phineas and Ferb*, who is always in a spin about something, screeching or giggling, depending on the situation.

Candace also showcases another demeaning aspect of fictional girlhood—the constant pursuit of male attention. While not common to all girls, it is evident in a variety of popular TV programs and films.

For her part, Candace is obsessed with her crush, Jeremy. Unlike her calm and collected paramour, Candace is always worried that he will lose interest and regularly goes to humiliating lengths to impress him. Isabella, also of *Phineas and Ferb*, is another love-struck female. The object of her affections is Phineas. She often participates in his schemes and equips herself well, but is motivated more by her attraction to Phineas than by any sense of adventure or fun.

On animated program *Johnny Test*, geniuses Susan and Mary swoon over their crush, Gil, even fainting when, in an attempt to use his "hotness" to melt snow, they get him to expose his upper body. In *Bakugan Battle Brawlers*, the girls get into occasional high-volume fights over the boys. The movie *Cars* features the Dinoco girls, who parade around the winner at the end of each race, and "the twins," female racing groupies who, in stereotypical boy-chasing fashion, quickly shift allegiances to whichever car happens to be winning. The "pollen jocks" from *Bee Movie* elicit a similar response from the female bees.

In the literary world, the princesses in *Sir Fartsalot Hunts the Booger* throw themselves at the knights who accompany lead male Prince Harry, blowing them kisses and sending them love notes, even though one of the knights is an elderly man. Even Geronimo Stilton gets plenty of attention from the females he knows, although he usually manages to turn them off with his silly behaviour.

By portraying girls as frivolous, overly emotional, and having few concerns other than appealing to boys, pop culture is aiding and abetting traditional views of masculinity. Because girls often relate only to the men in a story and are positioned as either lovesick schoolgirls or nagging wives/sisters/daughters, they reinforce the idea that females are of secondary importance to males and have little to offer beyond flirting with boys or making them miserable.

Troublesome Lessons About Masculinity

Pop culture is serving boys a steady diet of stereotyped male characters and creating a pecking order that sends clear messages about the worth of each type.

The negative lessons gleaned from these stereotypes and their positioning, relative to each other, are many. Boys learn that passivity and politeness are signs of weakness. They see that success comes from being aggressive and that vulnerability should be avoided. They also begin to recognize where they fit on the continuum of masculinity, with those who are closer to the bottom often attempting to compensate for their perceived lack of masculinity with false bravado. (Witness any boy who tries to stifle tears when upset or who "sucks it up" instead of admitting he is hurt.)

These lessons call to mind Levant's traditional definition of masculinity, which is in evidence all over the television dial, the silver screen, and bookshelves. In these fictional worlds, arrogant, brash alpha-males like Dan, Scott, and Dillon are held up as some sort of ideal in sharp contrast to "wimpy" smart guys like Marucho and clowns like Ziggy. Belligerence and violence are pervasive. Even those boys who possess some degree of sensitivity—like Ben Tennyson and Anakin Skywalker—turn into aggressive warriors when duty calls.

While it is often thought that gender stereotypes affect girls more than boys, professor of child development Susan D. Witt believes that stereotypes limit opportunities for both sexes. In her article "Parental influence on children's socialization to gender roles" Witt also discusses the many benefits associated with eliminating gender stereotypes: children raised in gender-neutral or androgynous environments tend to have higher self-esteem, more flexible attitudes towards sex roles, and "the knowledge that they have the ability to make choices which are not hindered by gender."[26]

This idea of not being hemmed in by gender is as relevant to boys as it is to girls. Stories about the trouble with boys, their poor performance at school, and their diminishing numbers in universities appear regularly in the news. While those problems are far too complex to have a single solution, a good first step would be an examination of how young boys are socialized and what they are being taught about masculinity.

Instead of allowing pop culture to tell boys that smart, studious boys are losers and that cool guys fight and break the rules, parents and caregivers should demand more nuanced portrayals of male characters. This does not mean a complete abandonment of traditional masculinity, but rather an acceptance of the idea that manliness does not mean brute force and a hair-trigger temper; it has a wider meaning and can encompass traits like intelligence, sensitivity, and compassion.

Chapter 2: Distant and Disappointed Dads: Pop Culture Lessons About Fatherhood

Watching the birth of Betty and Don Draper's third child on the 1960s-set television series *Mad Men*, I had to laugh at its portrayal of the way things used to be. Upon arrival at the hospital, Don assists Betty into a wheelchair and the nurse tells him: "Your job is done." He kisses Betty on the head then retires to the waiting room where he and another expectant father share a bottle of Johnnie Walker Red.

Fathers have come a long way since then, but pop culture is still clinging to an outdated and negative image of dads. The fathers in kids' popular culture are not necessarily Don Draper, but in their coolness and distance as parents, they are not that far removed from him.

Dads in children's movies and television are often depicted as cold fish—emotionally detached, physically distant, or unable to communicate with their children, especially if they are boys. They stand alongside the fathers in adult pop culture, who are often clownish figures, ridiculed or scolded by the women in their lives. In these narratives, Mom always seems to save the day when Dad's immaturity and lack of common sense land him or his children in hot water.

The impact of poor portrayals of fathers was discussed in a 2008 article in *Advertising Age*. Such depictions influence the perceptions that young people have of dads and convey the idea that fathers are not great parents. This impression affects both boys and girls, the authors say, teaching boys that fatherhood is not something to which they should aspire, and telling girls that a father is not necessary for their children.[1]

As Canada's Media Awareness Network notes, such messages may resonate more strongly with children who have no father figure in their life[2] to counter the negative portrayals presented in pop culture. With some 550,000 single-parent families headed by women in Canada[3] and 9.8 million in the United States,[4] the potential impact of these far-from-perfect fictional dads is significant.

When it comes to inept fictional fathers, Homer Simpson of *The Simpsons* is one of the first to come to mind. Like most fathers on television sitcoms, Homer is dimwitted, selfish, and incompetent. He also spends a lot of time away from his children, either at Moe's Tavern or in front of the TV, beer in hand.

Homer's highly exaggerated flaws are played for humour and geared toward an audience older than the one I am discussing here. While some early school-age boys may be familiar with *The Simpsons*, most are more attuned to other areas of popular culture where portrayals of fathers are less comical but equally damaging.

Men and Domesticity – Never the Twain Shall Meet

From an early age, boys see a dissociation between manhood and fatherhood, with toys being one of the first indicators that parenting is not a job for men. Despite the fact that many toddler boys show an interest in emulating their parents in tasks like diaper changes, bathing, and feeding a baby, baby dolls and accessories are marketed exclusively to girls in the commercials that children see and in the places that parents—the main purchasers of toys—are most likely to shop.

Commercials for baby dolls like Baby Alive and Little Mommy leave no doubt as to who should play with the dolls. The ads feature gentle music, lots of pink, and voiceovers by female announcers. The websites for national vendors Toys R Us Canada and Chapters/Indigo, which parents may use for gift ideas or actual shopping, include gender-segregated categories for "role play" or "make believe" toys. Anyone seeking a baby doll for their child must check the girls' sections, where such toys are prominent. None are listed in the boys' sections.

The same feminine focus exists on the website for the popular Corolle line of baby dolls. It is completely aimed at girls, with pictures and text showing and describing girls playing with their dolls. The only mention of a boy is in the Miss Corolle product line, where 3-year-old girls (who can presumably become nothing other than wives and mothers) are encouraged to act grown up and "get engaged to Nicolas."[5]

While the majority of customers looking for baby dolls may be shopping for girls, excluding boys from the messaging that surrounds these toys makes boys who want to play "daddy" or "house" seem like some kind of aberration. This message is picked up on by parents who are highly sensitive to the gender-appropriateness of the toys their sons play with.[6] The messages in television advertising are not lost on young boys either: the models used in advertising are very influential in shaping boys' ideas about gender roles and appropriate play. In fact, television advertising has been called one of "the most important teachers of gendered behaviors."[7] Seeing girls playing with dolls in commercials indicates that they are girls' toys and, as such, verboten for boys.

In the marketing behind make-believe toys for early school-age boys it is more of the same. Toys for boys focus on jobs done outside the home or some fantasy world of heroes, not domesticity and parenting. Boys can pretend to be firefighters, police officers, construction workers, farmers, Transformers, and knights (Jedi or medieval), but they are not encouraged to take care of baby, clean the house, buy groceries, or do any of the tasks typically associated with Mom. Housekeeping and child care role-playing toys are marketed only to girls. The message for older boys and the parents who buy their toys is the same as that for preschoolers: men and domesticity do not mix.

Picture books also help create the impression that fathers take a backseat to mothers when it comes to child care. In 2005, economics professor David A. Anderson and psychology professor Mykol Hamilton wrote "Gender role stereotyping of parents in children's picture books: the invisible father," an article about the phenomenon of the invisible father in children's picture books. Appearing in the journal *Sex Roles*, the article summarizes the results of their study into 200 picture books, including many award winners and bestsellers. The authors found that fathers appeared in only 47% of them. Even when fathers were present, they were in far fewer scenes than mothers. Babies were nurtured nearly ten times as often by mothers and older children nearly two times as often, and fathers were never shown feeding or kissing babies.

Anderson and Hamilton concluded that current picture books portray fathers as "stoic actors who [take] little part in the lives of their children," socializing children at important periods in their development and teaching them to devalue fathers as caregivers.[8] Their findings were supported by another study done in 2009 by Suzanne Flannery Quinn, senior lecturer of early childhood studies at Roehampton University in London, England. She found that five years after Anderson's and Hamilton's study, fathers were still nearly invisible in bestselling picture books.[9]

Indeed, Mom is the sole parent in many popular picture books, including still bestselling classics like *Cloudy with a Chance of Meatballs* (although Mom has Grandpa to help her), *Snowy Day*, *The Story of Ferdinand*, *The Cat in the Hat* (but not its sequel), and *Where the Wild Things Are*. Popular book series *Olivia* also shows a father who is clearly less involved with his children than their mother. (The *Olivia* television series and the books based on it involve the father more.) Back-to-school favourite *The Kissing Hand* features a mother reassuring her son before he heads off to school for the first time, and *Goodnight Moon* features a maternal character putting a young boy to bed.

For older boys, there has been some progress in the literary realm. Unlike the picture books Anderson, Hamilton, and Quinn examined, books aimed at the early school-age set often include dads who are actively involved with their children. Take, for example, Robert Munsch, who currently dominates the bestseller lists on Canada's online booksellers, Chapters/Indigo and Amazon.

Munsch probably needs no introduction. He is the author of such childhood staples as *A Promise is a Promise* and *The Paper Bag Princess*. Several treasuries of his work have also been published. His books are popular and fun to read, and offer kids a healthy mix of mothers and fathers depicted in ways that are decidedly rare in children's picture books. In a kitchen scene in *The Boy in The Drawer*, the father is shown preparing dinner while the mother sits at the kitchen table reading. In *Moira's Birthday*, Moira's father is just as involved as her mother in birthday party preparations. In *Look at Me*, the parents are shown with stereotypical interests—he in tools and she in kitchen implements—yet both are active in their daughter's life.

Other authors have also included good fathers in their stories. The popular *The Magic Tree House* series, although focused mainly on the children, includes references to both parents, as does the recently re-published *Barnes and the Brains* series. The *Quigleys* series by Simon Mason features a dad who works long hours and occasionally grumbles at his children, but still has a good relationship with them. (For other titles with positive portrayals of fathers, consult the Recommended Resources list in the final chapter of this book.)

While the invisible father is slowly becoming less of a problem in the world of children's literature, absentee fathers crop up in other areas, including television and film. Unlike mothers, whose absences tend not to be of their own choosing (as we will see in the next chapter), a father's disappearance tends to be caused more often by deliberate decisions he makes. Whether it is a divorce, his career, or some other circumstance that keeps him away, he becomes a remote figure with little or no impact on his children.

A recent example from the big screen is *Shrek the Third*. Shrek himself is less than thrilled at the prospect of becoming a dad, but he comes around at the end of the film. The father of heir-to-the-kingdom Arthur is the deadbeat in this film. Arthur tells Shrek that his father dropped him off at boarding school "the first chance he got and I never heard from him again."

In the case of male lead Andy in *Toy Story*, it is hard to know what to make of his father. Andy has an infant sister, so viewers can assume that there is a father in the picture, but he is neither seen nor mentioned in this film or either of its two sequels. In fact, *Toy Story 3* opens with photographs from milestones in Andy's life and his father is not in any of them.

The Oscar-winning film *Up* provides another take on the absentee father. It centres on Russell, the Wilderness Explorer, who has not spent much time in the wild. He tells his new friend and eventual father figure, Carl, that his father promised him a camping trip but never delivered. He goes onto explain that he has not seen much of his father since his parents divorced.

Russell is one badge away from his Senior Wilderness Explorer rank. As he tries to complete the requirements for this badge, he expresses his hope that his father will attend the ceremony to present him with his award. Russell gets his final badge but, naturally, his father does not make an appearance. Carl takes the place of Russell's father, arriving at the last minute to save the child the humiliation of standing on stage, fatherless, in stark contrast to the other boys whose beaming fathers are present. Russell's father, like many fictional divorced dads, is understood to be a cad who abandoned his son in favour of his new family.

On the small screen, both Ash and Brock in the popular *Pokemon* series saw their fathers depart to pursue their life's goals of becoming Pokemon trainers.

In all cases, the fathers either deliberately absent themselves from their sons' lives or, in the case of Andy, simply do not exist. The exclusion of fathers reinforces the idea that Mom is the dependable parent who will always be there when Dad shirks his parental responsibilities, as he often does in children's film and television.

Absenteeism is not the only problem facing fictional fathers. Dads who are present are often emotionally distant from their sons and sometimes even harshly critical of them. The callousness that marks many fictional father/son relationships seems to be less common in relationships between fathers and daughters. In films like *Mulan* and the critically acclaimed *Kiki's Delivery Service*, fathers are shown as affectionate and caring towards their daughters—quite unlike the fathers of the sons described below.

On *Power Rangers: RPM*, both Flynn and Scott (Rangers Blue and Red) have to prove themselves to critical fathers, although Scott has a much harder time of it. Flynn's father is exasperated by his son's inability to hold down a job, but swells with pride when Flynn proves himself a hero by rescuing a busload of people. Scott's dad is a stoic military man who continually underestimates his son's abilities as a soldier. His severe judgment of his son may stem from a desire to hold Scott back so he will not suffer the same fate as his older brother, who died in a military battle. But the father's decision to hide his true feelings behind harsh criticism places a strain on his relationship with his son, and leaves Scott bitter and angry.

The discord between Scott and his father is not uncommon in fictional father/son relationships, where tension between parent and child is frequently based in the father's disappointment in his son.

In some of the most popular children's movies of recent years, fathers have criticized, expressed their frustration, and even disowned their sons for failing to live up to their high standards. Yet such portrayals typically go unnoticed in commentary about the films, suggesting that these kinds of exchanges between fathers and sons are normal or even expected.

Fantastic Mr. Fox is one of the latest films to cover this ground. It is an entertaining film, but the relationship between Mr. Fox and his son Ash is troubling.

In the book on which the film is based, none of Fox's children are named. To add depth to the movie, writer/director Wes Anderson added a little family drama via Ash and his visiting cousin, Kristofferson. Ash is, as everyone in the film notes, "different," a term that seems to imply "nerdy." His unique personality leads to conflicts with his father who, when Kristofferson arrives, immediately falls to comparing his clumsy, smallish son to his far more athletic cousin. He even goes so far as to tell Ash that he is "too little and uncoordinated" to participate in his scheme to steal food from the local farmers.

Mr. Fox, through his sometimes harsh disapproval of his son, implies that Ash is less masculine and of less worth than his cousin because he cannot dive or play "Whack-Bat" as well. Other characters seem to agree. Ash is told by a bully that he "dresses like a girl." When Ash tells Kristofferson he can fight his own fights, his cousin tells him, "No you can't."

Eventually Ash and his father have the heart-to-heart chat that is de rigueur in kids' films, in which Dad tells his son he loves him, in a roundabout fashion. Ash later proves himself to his still doubting father, who had assigned him to cleaning duty instead of inviting him to help rescue the kidnapped Kristofferson. When Ash takes a risk and saves the day, his father tells him his actions were "pure, wild animal craziness" and that he is "an athlete," implying that he finally views Ash as equal to his cousin. A happy ending to be sure, yet the lasting image for me—and I'm sure for at least a few young viewers—is that of a young boy, yearning for approval, and being told by his father that he doesn't measure up.

Reviewers of this film have noted that the fractious father/son relationship is a recurring theme in Wes Anderson's movies, but he is not the only one to explore this territory in a children's film.

The lighthearted *Happy Feet* includes not one but two bad fathers. First, there is Memphis, the father of Mumble, the penguin who can dance but not sing. (The ability to sing is, according to this film, essential to penguins.) Memphis is ashamed of his son, telling him that dancing "just ain't penguin." When Mumble is banished from the colony, his father says nothing. He merely nods his head in agreement with the exile. Second is the father of Ramon, one of Mumble's newfound friends from outside his colony. Although his father is not seen in the film, Ramon notes that his dad once called him "a pitiful loser." (Contrast Ramon's father to Kiki's dad, who calls her "my little princess" in *Kiki's Delivery Service*.)

The fathers in both *Fantastic Mr. Fox* and *Happy Feet* stand in stark contrast to the mother characters. In the former, Mrs. Fox gently tells her son that the things that make him different also make him special.

In the latter, mother Norma Jean stands steadfastly by her son despite his far-from-perfect singing voice. Harsh words would never be expected from either Mrs. Fox or Norma Jean, but in their husbands and other father characters, they are considered acceptable. This juxtaposition of mothers and fathers implies that fathers are naturally poorer parents—too tough, too emotionally distant, and too quick to find fault with sons who are different.

Even in films where there is no mother character to balance the father's coldness, the message is the same.

In *Ratatouille*, Remy the gourmand with the hyper-sensitive nose frustrates his father because he is so unlike the other rats in their colony. They like to scrounge for garbage while Remy would prefer to cook and indulge his taste for fine cuisine. His father is dismissive of Remy's olfactory talent, saying: "So you can smell ingredients? So what?" Remy counters this statement by saying that his father is "never impressed," signalling a sort of resignation that his father will never value his unique skills. While Remy's father is not as hostile as his counterparts in other films, his disapproval of his son's interests creates some friction between them.

Then there is the rather puzzling case of the 2010 release, *How to Train Your Dragon*. It is the story of a boy named Hiccup who is, like Mumble and Remy, different from his tribe. As noted in the previous chapter, in the print version of the story, Hiccup is called useless by the other boys and considered unremarkable in just about every way. While not without its flaws, the book presents Hiccup's father in a good light. He knows his son is not like the other boys, but he clearly loves him and accepts him for who he is.

The animated version of the story is quite unlike the book. Hiccup's father, Stoick the Vast, is frustrated by his son. He views him as disaster waiting to happen. He bemoans the fact that Hiccup is so different from the fierce group of dragon killers that inhabit their village. When Stoick discovers that Hiccup actually likes dragons and prefers to domesticate them rather than kill them, he virtually disowns him, telling him: "You are not my son." It is only when the entire tribe is at risk and Hiccup takes it upon himself to save everyone (and prove that he is a real man) that Stoick tells his son he is proud of him.

In the film *The Tale of Despereaux*, the father also abandons the son. When the titular mouse is found to have broken the laws of his tribe by talking to a human, he is punished by being dropped down a sewer vent where it is believed he will be killed by rats. How was his crime discovered? His father, who had been very patient towards his son's differences until that point, alerted the authorities to his son's transgressions. Despereaux's father is hopeful that he and his wife can secure a light sentence, but when the boy's banishment is announced, he does not ask the authorities to be lenient; he merely tells his sobbing wife that there is nothing to be done, expressing no remorse and no regret.

In all cases, the fathers and sons reconcile their differences in the end, but not before the son is cast out or made to feel ashamed of who he really is by the one man who should support and protect him—his father.

Outcasts abound in children's entertainment, going back as far as a certain red-nosed reindeer who brought shame to his father. While conflict between the lead protagonist and another character drives the narrative, it seems the father is always the heavy. Mothers come across as angelic compared to their husbands, who are made to appear insensitive and unduly concerned with their sons' ability to conform to social norms.

If it is not disappointment that separates fathers and sons, it is a lack of communication. (This failure to communicate should come as no surprise, I suppose, since men, according to stereotype, do not like to talk about their feelings.)

Tim in *Cloudy with a Chance of Meatballs* is father to Flint, the inventor of the machine that turns weather systems into food. Although he does not appear to be a cold-hearted man, Tim's inability to speak openly to his son causes problems between them and leaves his son feeling unloved. Only after Flint nearly loses his life can his father express himself. Even then, he needs an intermediary—a machine that Flint invented to translate monkey babbling into human speech. Not exactly a great metaphor for father/son relationships.

In *Kung Fu Panda*, the lack of communication results in the father being oblivious to his son's true nature. Lead male Po's goal is to become a kung fu master, but he cannot find the nerve to tell his father, Mr. Ping, a gentle and caring parent who hopes that his son will follow him into the noodle business. When Po's chance to fulfill his dream and become a hero fizzles out, his father remains in denial about his son's ambition and brushes off his disappointment. Mr. Ping tells Po that his dream was not meant to be and that he should forget it because his destiny awaits him in the noodle business.

Both Tim and Mr. Ping love their sons—a trait that is not readily apparent in some of the other fathers discussed here—but their inability to communicate diminishes them as parents. This lack of communication is intended to add dramatic tension, but it also underscores the notion that talking, expressing emotions, and making an effort to understand one another are things that fathers and sons do not do, even if their relationship is jeopardized by their refusal to connect in any meaningful way.

Mr. Ping's kind and patient nature does not improve his parenting skills, but it does differentiate him from the gruff dads that are so common in kids' pop culture. There are other exceptions and together these characters offer some hope that depictions of fathers will change. *Finding Nemo* includes a father who is nurturing and caring. *The Incredibles* centres on a two-parent family with an involved father who gets distracted by his work and his calling as a superhero, but never forgets his family. Animated film *Everyone's Hero* shows two caring and engaged fathers—one the father of lead male Yankee and the other the father to Marti, the girl who helps Yankee. In the popular TV show *Phineas and Ferb*, the parents leave frequently to pursue their own interests (and advance the plot), but there is no doubt that the children enjoy a healthy relationship with both Mom and Dad. And in *Johnny Test*, parental roles are reversed with Dad being the stay-at-home parent and Mom being the breadwinner.

Even *Bakugan Battle Brawlers*, far from a trailblazer as far as gender is concerned, shows two-parent families on the few occasions when parents are involved in the plot. Characters like Marucho, Dan, and Runo all have a mom and dad at home and the fathers seem involved to at least some degree in the lives of their children.

Men First, Fathers Second

What impact does the Y-chromosome have on a man's ability to parent? Apparently, it makes him uncommunicative, emotionally and sometimes physically distant, and too career-oriented to build a proper relationship with his children.

It is no coincidence that the traits shared by the far-from-perfect fictional fathers I described here align exactly with the characteristics of the ideal man: stoic, independent from emotional attachments, and focused on status and success. Fathers in children's pop culture are, after all, men first and parents second.

As such, they further entrench conventional ideas about manhood while reinforcing traditional gender roles, teaching young boys to view fathers as incompetent or uncaring parents, and perpetuating the notion that child care and domestic chores are best left to the woman of the house.

Chapter 3: Separating Boys from their Mothers' Influence

Since fictional fathers are often cast as bad parents, it is reasonable to assume that mothers would be exalted in children's popular culture. While some are held up as ideal parents, especially in comparison to fathers, many more are removed from their sons' lives altogether and replaced by a male father figure. This rejection of mothers is evidence of a belief that strong feminine influence leaves a boy "soft, weak, dependent, [and] homebound,"[1] a notion that has emerged as a narrative thread in stories throughout history.

In *The Courage to Raise Good Men*, Olga Silverstein and Beth Rashbaum cite many examples from popular culture—from ancient myths to the present day—in which boys are separated "from the sphere of the mother" so they can be raised as real men.[2] The story of Achilles and his mother is among them.

Achilles' mother, Thetis, is a stereotypical overprotective mother. Her efforts to shield her son from the premature death that the Prophecy foretold began in infancy with that infamous dip in the River Styx, and continued during the Trojan War when she disguised Achilles as a maiden to keep him from fighting. Because she tried to prevent her son from fulfilling his manly duty as a soldier and, worse still, humiliated him by forcing him to dress like a girl, Thetis was presented as a threat to her son's manhood in the stories that emerged from that period.

In the *The Achilleid*, the poet Statius notes that Achilles' mentor Chiron would never have given the boy back to Thetis if he had known her "dishonourable" intentions. Achilles and Ulysses also have harsh words for Thetis. Ulysses describes her actions with words like "fraud and cunning" and refers to her as a "crafty mother" who "profaned" her son with feminine clothing. He also notes that she is "anxious" and "timorous" and "too true a mother." Achilles admits that he felt shame for having "served a timid lord" and refers to his "mother's crime" and the "dishonourable robe" he was made to wear.[3]

Given their deeply misogynistic society, it is no surprise that Thetis was depicted as she was. In the words of journalist and writer Jack Holland, the ancient Greeks may have been the "colonists of our intellectual world," but they were also the "intellectual pioneers of a pernicious view of women" that began with the story of Pandora and continued with the stories of mythical warriors like Achilles and his contemporaries.[4]

While we have come a long way since then, the mindset that saw Thetis cast as a meddling, negative influence on her son underlies many of today's films and television shows—even those aimed at school-age children—where the separation of mothers and sons is a frequent occurrence. Once separated from their mothers, these boys, like Achilles, are often taken under the wing of a male mentor, reinforcing the idea that women, with their supposedly gentle and passive nature, are not up to the job of turning boys into men.

From Achilles to Anakin:
The Absence of Maternal Influence

They are worlds away from each other but Achilles and *Star Wars* hero Anakin Skywalker share similar childhood experiences: both are taken from their mothers at a young age and groomed as warriors by a male father figure.

As fictional characters go, Achilles and Anakin are not alone. The kind of break experienced by these two heroes is surprisingly common in children's film and, to some extent, television. Boys are routinely separated from their mothers and, in most cases, left without female influence in their young lives.

In one typical narrative arc, the breaking of the bond between mother and son is permanent—she either dies or simply doesn't exist. Examples of this type of mother/son separation emerge consistently in all genres of film and animated television shows. Even in lighter entertainment, where one might not expect to find such a serious theme, the death rate for mothers is remarkably high.

The comedy *Ice Age* is one example. The film revolves around a baby who is found and cared for by animals before being returned to his family, minus one member. In the opening minutes of the film, the baby's mother quietly slips into the water after handing her son to the lead character—a woolly mammoth who recently lost his wife and child—and is never heard from or mentioned again. A similar fate is suffered by Nemo's mother, who is eaten by a barracuda early in the film *Finding Nemo*. In *Cloudy with a Chance of Meatballs*, the mother of male lead Flint also dies after the opening scenes of the film and misses seeing her son complete his greatest invention.

The creators of the 2010 release *How to Train Your Dragon* took this trend one step further by deliberately excising the mother of lead male Hiccup, who was present in the book on which the film is based. Her absence is noted in a scene between father and son in which the elder man presents his son with a helmet made from his deceased wife's breastplate. Both father and son are saddened at her death, but the scene is ultimately played for laughs when Hiccup shows his distaste for the helmet. (He does wear the helmet later.)

*why bad – appeal
to kids   Sans mother
        it's not
        super
        common*

In some cases, the mother character is not acknowledged in any way and can only be presumed dead. In *Shrek the Third*, future king Arthur talks about the father who abandoned him but never discusses his mother. Remy from *Ratatouille* complains about his dad but makes no reference to his mom, and in *Kung Fu Panda*, lead male Po's mother is not mentioned. In *Barnyard*, Otis the male cow shows up "stumbling around," presumably just born, and is adopted by another male cow named Ben. In recounting his tale of finding Otis, Ben mentions nothing of the calf's mother.

On the action/adventure side, there is also a decided lack of maternal influence. Two of the four male Power Rangers are orphaned, while two have fathers but no mother to speak of. Solitary warrior Shun in *Bakugan Battle Brawlers* watches his mother die after a long illness, an event that causes him sadness but eventually leads him back to his warrior games. Abandoned by his father, Brock from *Pokemon* is also motherless, but in a unique twist, takes it upon himself to become the parent for his younger siblings.

While death is certainly the most effective means of separating mothers and sons, it is not the only way the bond is broken. Sometimes the mother distances herself from her son. This separation, whether entered into willingly by the mother or pushed on her by her son, is depicted as something that she should welcome as a sign of her son's maturity and desire for independence.

In the case of critically acclaimed film *Ponyo*, the separation is initiated by the mother. While not permanent, it is difficult for the boy in question. In this film, a monster tsunami threatens a small Japanese city, yet the scene that proved most troubling to many young viewers had nothing to do with the storm. With the waters raging around his home, five-year-old Sosuke is left behind by his mother. Her reasons are noble—she works at a seniors' home and wants to check on the residents—but her son is scared and upset. Still, she departs amidst his tears and protests, telling him that he is the man of the house and that even though he is young, he can take care of himself and his new friend Ponyo. Sosuke is a very positive male character—smart, sensitive, and gentle—and it is unsettling to see him cast so abruptly into the role of "man" by his mother. He returns to her later, but only after an emotional rollercoaster precipitated by her belief that a young boy could be man enough to fend for himself in a frightening and dangerous situation. One wonders if she would have done the same if her child were a girl.

Separation is the son's idea in the television show *Pokemon*. Ten-year-old Ash decides to leave his mother in order to fulfill his dream of being a Pokemon trainer. She breaks down in tears at his departure, causing him some embarrassment, but accepts that his journey is necessary. When Ash feels overwhelmed by his mission and calls his mother, she, in an act of motherly denial, does not talk about missing him or ask him to return home. She instead reassures him that he is on the right path with a speech about him spreading his wings and flying.

Colony politics force the separation of Mumble from his family in *Happy Feet*, but he shows no sign of concern when he is banished. As he is about to leave, his mother begins to say something and he stops her, saying, "It's okay mom," a simple statement that signifies his readiness to venture into the world without his family.

Current popular culture also gives us a hero whose story manages to interweave both types of mother/son narrative—dramatic separation followed by death.

Star Wars: Episode 1: The Phantom Menace introduces Anakin Skywalker, a child endowed with the "force" that all Jedi possess. Discovered by the Jedi, Anakin leaves his mother, Shmi, to begin his education. He is excited at the prospect of becoming a Jedi, but saddened at the thought of leaving his mother, who is a slave and cannot travel. After a tender good-bye during which he promises to free her, she tells him to be brave and not look back, knowing that his departure is for the best. In the film's sequel, subtitled *Attack of the Clones*, Shmi dies in Anakin's arms after having endured weeks of torture. She dies happy, having toughed it out long enough to see her son one last time, and saying with her last breath that she now felt "complete."[5] (In the new animated series *Star Wars: The Clone Wars*, the murder is not discussed explicitly, but it is revealed that Anakin is scarred by a tragic secret involving his homeland and family.)

While the fathers of male characters occasionally die or leave as well, there is one critical difference: they are replaced. Male friends and mentors abound for a young boy separated from his family, but women are never inserted into the story to take the place of the lost mother.

Consider *Ice Age*, where the male baby enjoys a long sojourn with the all-male cast before being reunited with his father, or *Finding Nemo*, where Nemo interacts with a group consisting almost entirely of males before finding his father. Remy of *Ratatouille* is separated from his father, but finds friendship and his life's purpose with a male chef-in-training who has, coincidentally, recently lost his mother. Like Nemo, Remy reconnects with his father near the end of the film. Exiled penguin Mumble also finds solace in a group of male friends before returning to his colony.

Beyond companionship, many male characters find male mentors to guide them toward their destiny. Male kung fu masters Shifu and Oogway train Po in *Kung Fu Panda*. Brock teaches Ash about catching and training Pokemon. Obi-Wan Kenobi raises Anakin Skywalker to be a Jedi knight. Hiccup in the film *How to Train Your Dragon* has a fractious relationship with his father, but finds something of a mentor in dragon hunting trainer, Gobber. Young cow Otis is seemingly abandoned by his mother in *Barnyard* and then adopted by kind and gentle Ben. Bruce Wayne loses his parents when he is young and is raised by his father's butler Alfred, a man he continues to depend on even after he becomes Batman.

The film *Up* also emphasizes the importance of male influence on boys. As I mentioned in the previous chapter, the parents of male protagonist Russell are divorced. As the movie progresses, the audience learns that Russell's father has virtually disappeared from his life. Following a familiar pattern, Russell finds an older male to replace his missing father and it is this man, Carl, who attends the all-important Wilderness Explorer awards ceremony in place of Russell's father.

Where is Russell's mother? Sitting in the audience, quietly clapping for her son. That she is excluded from the ceremony speaks volumes about how her relationship with her son is to be interpreted. She is the caretaker and the go-to parent, but she is not enough. She must give way to a virtual stranger and allow him to become a second parent to her son.

In pointing out these instances of mother denial (in the words of Silverstein and Rashbaum), I am not discounting the importance of a male role model in a boy's life; I am questioning why, in children's popular culture, a male role model can only come at the expense of the mother.

Of course, mothers are not treated shabbily in all children's entertainment—*Toy Story* and *Happy Feet* both include close mother/son relationships—but, as the examples I have included here demonstrate, it is not at all uncommon to see mothers disposed of or cut out of their sons' lives in some way. That this narrative thread is seen in some of the most popular stories and across all genres in children's film and television—comedy, sci-fi, superhero, and adventure—only underscores how pervasive a theme it is.

To uncover exactly why this theme of mother/son separation appears with such regularity, we need only look at the tenets of traditional masculinity. These masculine imperatives are reflected in popular culture, telling boys that they must be stoic and emotionally detached, they need to present themselves at all times as strong and independent, and they must avoid all things feminine[A break with Mom accomplishes all of these things, leaving fictional boys free to become the real men they are destined to be.] ✳

The concept of detachment is especially relevant to boys. As the International Central Institute for Youth and Educational Television (IZI) noted in a 2008 report, children's television places tremendous value on the separation of a boy or man from emotional attachments, traditions, and his background.[6] The break between a son and his mother—carried out by choice or by force—is the ultimate detachment from home and family. [It is also presented as a desirable and necessary first step on a boy's journey toward manhood.) Whether the separation is caused by a death, a tropical storm, or a wayward youngster who finds himself lost and alone, the message is the same—boys need to be removed from the comforts of home and the sometimes suffocating attentions of Mom in order to become men.

As I noted in the introduction, the imperative to act manly affects boys from a very young age. Dislike of physical affection, feigning toughness, embarrassment about crying—all are ways that young boys try to demonstrate their manhood. This compulsion to act traditionally masculine stems, in part, from the association between feminine behaviour and weakness—an association that is reinforced throughout children's pop culture.

Of course, the notion that boys must be separated from all things feminine and domestic, lest they place their manhood at risk, is not just apparent in TV and film. Toys and the marketing behind them send the same message, loud and clear.

Studies into what constitutes a typical boy's or girl's toy date back to the mid-70s. In 2005, psychologists Judith E. Owen Blakemore and Renee E. Centers decided to update this research to see how today's toys fare on the gender scale. Done in two parts, their study "Characteristics of boys' and girls' toys," which appeared in the journal *Sex Roles*, showed which modern toys are considered to be for boys and which for girls. It then rated these toys based on a standardized set of characteristics, like violence, educational value, and cognitive skills.

Unsurprisingly, strongly feminine toys scored high for encouraging nurturing and domestic or household skills. Strongly masculine toys were rated at the bottom for these same characteristics.[7] A look at Canadian online toy sellers corroborates what was found in the study.

Under the category of "Girl's Pretend Play and Dress-Up" on the Toys R Us Canada website are sub-categories for kitchens and household appliances, shopping carts and registers, and dollhouses. Shoppers looking at the "Boy's Role Play" category are led to magic sets, Home Depot toy tools, and costumes running the gamut from medieval knights to S.W.A.T team members, soldiers, *Star Wars* and *Transformers* characters, and WWE wrestlers, with nary a kitchen or cooking implement in sight.[8]

Chapters/Indigo has a similar gender divide in its make-believe section. Girls' make-believe toys include baking and decorating sets, baby dolls and accessories, kitchens, and café sets. For boys? Fire trucks, construction vehicles, airports, farm vehicles, railways, knights, and tools.[9] (Gender differences are not so stark on the site for Grand River Toys, which includes food and kitchen stuff for boys, or on that of Mastermind Toys, which does not divide toys by sex.)

There is one area of popular culture where fictional moms and sons seem to enjoy a decent relationship—books.

In picture books, the closeness between mothers and sons comes at a cost to fathers, who are shown as less involved with their children: women are 3 ½ times more likely than men to perform nurturing behaviours, like child care, and nearly twice as many male characters are shown working outside the home, marginalizing them as parents.[10] Aforementioned classics, like *The Story of Ferdinand, Cloudy with a Chance of Meatballs*, and *Where the Wild Things Are* are just some of the examples of stories that feature mothers as solo parents. (Some titles, like *Love You Forever* by the otherwise reliable Robert Munsch, go too far in their depiction of the mother/son relationship. Although beloved by many parents, that title has raised the ire of some adult readers who consider it an example of the smothering mother trope described by Silverstein and Rashbaum.)

In books for older boys, there are also plenty of moms around. Other titles by Robert Munsch, the *Stink* series by Megan McDonald, *Barnes and the Brains*, and the *Fudge* series by Judy Blume all include mothers interacting with their sons, albeit with Dad having a strong presence.

The circle, then, while not quite complete, is nearly so. Films, television, and toys all work together to reinforce the idea that males should be removed from maternal influence and any associated feminine behaviours. Books provide something of a counterbalance for mother/ son relationships, but the frequent omission of the father character in picture books indicates that in the literary realm, the pendulum can swing too far the other way.

And what of boys who enjoy a close relationship with a mother character? There are definite consequences, at least in the eyes of some TV producers.

In an episode of *SpongeBob SquarePants* entitled "Grandma's Kisses," SpongeBob is mercilessly ridiculed by his friends for receiving a kiss on the forehead from his grandmother. He is called "Grandma's boy" and a "big baby who wears diapers." He is told that he's "a man now" and should start acting like one. Even though he eventually accepts that he can be an adult and still kiss his grandmother, he asks her not to tell his friends.

The world of superheroes also gives us some subtle clues as to the fate of "Mama's boys." Among the alter egos of the more popular superheroes, those with maternal influence in their lives are depicted as less manly. Peter Parker (Spider-Man), who lives with his Aunt May, is widely considered to be a geek. Clark Kent, who lives with his adoptive parents, is also a nerd, at least until he dons his Superman garb. Peter and Clark stand in contrast to the aforementioned Bruce Wayne, who disguises his heroic side behind the image of a wealthy playboy, and the motorcycle-riding, scowling alpha-male Logan, a.k.a. Wolverine.

Mother Denial

In frequently discounting the importance of mothers and telling boys that a break from Mom is a sign of strength and maturity, current popular culture is introducing an entirely new generation of boys to the idea that femininity is anathema to men.

Like the stereotypes of women that dominate popular culture, this discarding of mothers also serves to denigrate women, making them seem, at best, irrelevant to their sons and, at worst, a threat to their impending manhood. That a dead or deliberately diminished mother is replaced by a man sends an equally negative message, positioning men as more valuable than women, especially in the highly important task of transforming a young boy into a man.

Chapter 4: Male Dominance and Lack of Female Heroes

Women in North America make up more than half the population, but young boys immersed in popular culture would never know it. In TV shows and films aimed at a mixed audience—that is, programs that do not involve a Barbie or a princess—the protagonists are nearly always male.

With the action and main plotlines reserved for boys and men, girls and women are relegated to the background. Even those who are considered strong female role models suffer in today's entertainment. While they may possess some wonderful traits—like bravery, courage, and intelligence—they are rarely afforded the opportunity to be anything more than a wife or girlfriend.

To many observers, male dominance may seem to be a bigger problem for girls than boys. In creating the impression that being male is the norm and that females are "the other" or the "second sex" (in the words of Simone de Beauvoir), this emphasis on the male experience lowers girls' self-esteem and occupational aspirations.[1] But I would argue that a males-only focus also has an impact on boys.

The imbalance between male and female characters gives boys a "biased representation of the social world"[2] that promotes gender inequality while reinforcing many of the stereotypes discussed earlier: men are the stronger sex and, as such, cannot betray signs of femininity or weakness; men are protectors and must show their strength and aggression when needed; and men are natural leaders who must aspire to be in charge.

These lessons might be countered to some degree by a boy's day-to-day existence, but the culture that surrounds him and the mythology that emerges from it are distinctly male. From *Ben 10* to *Star Wars* and from *Cars* to *Toy Story*, male achievement is the focal point of children's popular culture and the female experience is, for the most part, entirely absent.

Kids' Pop Culture: The World Revolves Around Men

Although a study is probably not necessary to prove the prevalence of male characters in kids' entertainment, the numbers may surprise even the most gender-conscious parent.

A 2008 paper by the International Central Institute for Youth and Educational Television (IZI) found that only 32% of main characters in children's television are female. In animated programs, that discrepancy can go as high as 87% male to 13% female.[3] The numbers in films are similar. A study sponsored by the Geena Davis Institute on Gender in Media (GDIGM), also released in 2008, shows that in G-rated films released between 1990 and 2005, only 28% of speaking characters are female.

This situation shows no sign of improving. Looking at the statistics from a historical perspective, the GDIGM researchers found that the numbers remained constant over the sixteen years studied—there was neither an increase nor a decrease in the number of female characters.[4]

Indeed. Think of the most recognizable animated big-screen characters from the past few years (with the exception of princess movies). The list consists entirely of males:

- Carl and Russell, the lonely senior and little boy from *Up*.
- Po from *Kung Fu Panda*.
- Flint from *Cloudy with a Chance of Meatballs*.
- Lightning McQueen, the hotshot race car in *Cars*.
- Mumble, the dancing penguin from *Happy Feet*.
- Shrek, the ogre from the *Shrek* series of films.
- Remy, the rat with a taste for fine cuisine in *Ratatouille*.
- Nemo, the lost little clownfish from the movie *Finding Nemo*.
- Manny and Sid from the *Ice Age* series.
- Mike and Sully, the monsters who get saddled with a human toddler in *Monsters, Inc.*
- Otis and Ben, father and son protagonists from *Barnyard*.
- Woody and Buzz Lightyear, the toys from the *Toy Story* franchise who are owned by little boy Andy.

It is not just the presence of a male protagonist that signifies male dominance. The preference for male characters extends to the supporting characters who accompany the lead male throughout the film.

Consider just a few examples. In the first *Ice Age* film, there are no females among the group of characters that rescue the infant human. The group of kung fu masters encountered by Po in *Kung Fu Panda* includes strong females but they have a negligible impact on the story—Po learns his most valuable lessons from the two older male masters and his father. Mumble, the dancing penguin from *Happy Feet*, finds companionship with a group of male Adelie penguins after he is cast out of his colony. Remy the rat mentors the male chef Linguini and finds inspiration in male chef Auguste Gusteau. Woody and Buzz Lightyear are surrounded almost entirely by male toys, including Mr. Potato Head, Slinky Dog, Rex the dinosaur, and Hamm the pig. In *Barnyard*, a film that tells the story of a group of partying farm animals and has spawned an animated TV series, most of the "cows" are male.

Cloudy with a Chance of Meatballs is something of an exception. Sam Sparks, the female weather reporter, has a major role in the film and even comes close to playing the part of hero, but she is the only female with any degree of involvement in the film. Flint's mother has minimal screen time before she dies, and every other character with a speaking part is male: Flint's father, the mayor, the police chief, the police chief's son, camera operator Manny, town celebrity Brent, and Flint's simian sidekick, Steve.

Not only are females fewer in number and less influential in most films, when they are present, they are often shown in traditional roles. Research done by the forerunner to the GDIGM, an organization called See Jane, noted the occupations of characters in children's films. The most common jobs for females were: clerical and secretarial, entertainment, and royalty. Females were also far more likely to be married or parents. The top three types of employment for men were white collar, blue collar, and military.[5]

According to most popular kids' films, it seems boys can aspire to be king, business leader, police chief, or army general. Girls can be secretary to any of these guys or a princess (not queen) and, almost always, somebody's mom.

Fiona from the *Shrek* series is a case in point. *Shrek the Third* begins with a protracted scene in which Princess Fiona's father is shown on his deathbed. As king, he must ensure that his successor is in place but the notion that Fiona could be queen is not mentioned. In the land of Far, Far Away the throne is passed from Fiona's father to either her husband or another male heir.

Fiona is a good example of where female characters rate in kids' popular culture, as is Ellie from the *Ice Age* franchise. By merely being present, they add some degree of balance to their respective film series.

But presence does not always mean progress. Like many of the female characters who are starting to populate other kids' films, Fiona and Ellie are recognized primarily as the love interests of the leading males. As such, their place in the narrative is well-defined. Each can stand behind her man and inspire him with her bravery and courage, but neither can surpass him and become more heroic or important than him. The stories of Fiona, Ellie, and several others demonstrate how often females are kept in the wife/girlfriend role and out of the hero role.

After Shrek is captured in *Shrek the Third*, Princess Fiona decides to lead the other princesses in a fight to rescue him, but the women do not act alone. They are accompanied by the other male characters, including Donkey and Puss-in-Boots. Upon bursting into the place where Shrek is being held, they promptly get captured themselves. It is Arthur and Shrek who ultimately disarm and capture the evil Prince Charming.

Ellie from *Ice Age 3* encourages her husband and his male friends to head into the dangerous world of dinosaurs to rescue their friend Sid, despite the potential risks and despite the fact that she is pregnant. Because Ellie goes into labour just as the real rescue effort is to begin, she cannot help save her friend. Instead, she has to stay back to bear a child. Assuming that she needs their help, two males stay behind with her and also miss out on the rescue, but the message is similar to what is seen in *Shrek the Third*—women can be brave, but saving lives is a job more suited to men.

In *Toy Story 2*, females are represented by Bo-Peep, who flirts with male lead Woody, and Mrs. Potato Head, who is married to her male counterpart. Neither of them get much screen time. When it comes time to rescue the kidnapped Woody, the male characters are the only ones who venture out into the world. For her part, Mrs. Potato Head provides a memorable example of wifely stereotypes, taking care to pack up everything her husband needs and wanting to adopt the little alien dolls that return home with him.

The film *Cars* follows the travails of a somewhat arrogant race car named Lightning McQueen, who finds himself stranded in a small town. During his stay in the town he learns some valuable life lessons from male character Doc Hudson and female Sally. McQueen and Sally eventually fall in love but her lower status is made clear when McQueen returns to the track for a climactic race with Doc and the other men from the town, leaving Sally behind with the other women to watch the race on television.

Colette, the only female chef (and the only female character) in *Ratatouille*, is the assigned mentor for Linguini, but she has little impact. It is Remy the rat who teaches Linguini how to cook. Although she is initially hostile to Linguini, Colette later falls for him.

In *Cloudy with a Chance of Meatballs*, the super-smart Samantha finds herself increasingly attracted to lead male Flint. She helps him get to his out-of-control food making machine high up in the sky, but is forced by a peanut allergy to leave him before their mission is completed. He ultimately saves the day on his own.

And then there is tough-as-nails Astrid in *How to Train Your Dragon*. She is the best dragon hunter in her class and does not suffer fools. In the beginning, she belittles and even physically fights with male lead Hiccup, but later becomes frightened when flying on a dragon with him. To comfort herself she nuzzles close to him and eventually develops feelings for him. In the battle that ends the film, Astrid plays a small part, but it is Hiccup who saves the day.

While many of these females are strong characters, the fact that they routinely fall in love with the male leads—occasionally with little reason to—diminishes their value and leaves the impression that they are token characters. They add some level of female presence but ultimately end up in a position of weakness, swooning over a man, willingly giving up their independence and, in cases like Colette and Astrid, softening their edgy and assertive natures for the sake of love.

Fortunately, there are a few films that offer a counterbalance to the conventional story arc that is so common in children's movies.

A rare female lead in an action film, Susan in *Monsters vs. Aliens* begins the movie as a stereotypical bride-to-be who is so smitten with her fiancé that she cannot see how selfish he is. Throughout the course of the movie, she discovers her own strengths and realizes she can achieve great things without him. This movie is not without its flaws. Male characters dominate, especially in the presidential war room where a timorous woman repeatedly drops the tray of coffee she is serving to the men, but the negative messages are outweighed to a great degree by the inclusion of a female protagonist who recognizes that she has value beyond being a wife or girlfriend.

The most identifiable characters in the film and TV series *Star Wars: The Clone Wars* are the males Anakin Skywalker, Obi-Wan Kenobi, Yoda and, on the Dark Side, Count Dooku. Yet females are heavily involved in the plot and in the marketing surrounding the film. Ahsoka Tano is a young woman, but a very capable fighter who saves Anakin's life and fends off three enemy soldiers by herself before completing the mission assigned to her. Her final battle is a refreshing change from most kids' films where females are typically rescued by a male character. Ahsoka is also pictured as part of the team in posters and other merchandise and is included in the toys based on the film.

Other females in the film and the television series spun off from it include Ventress, the fierce former Jedi who joined the Dark Side, and Luminara, a Jedi master. Senator Amidala is also a strong character, although on the animated series she is occasionally shown in need of rescue by Anakin, her secret love interest. There are others, too numerous to mention here. Some thirty-four female characters are listed in the *Star Wars: The Clone Wars Character Encyclopedia* and they include senators, a queen, bounty hunters, criminally minded shape-shifters, a "brilliant Republic scientist," and even astromech droids like R4-P17, who acts as co-pilot for Obi-Wan Kenobi.[6] This range of female characters, from soldiers to political leaders to villains, shows boys and girls that females can take on diverse roles outside the home.

Women also play an important part in *The Incredibles*. The film centres on Mr. Incredible, his wife, their daughter, and two sons. They are a family of superheroes forced by the government to live as normal people until Mr. Incredible is lured back into his superhero role, unleashing a set of circumstances that makes his family follow suit. Mrs. Incredible, better known as Elastigirl, has quick wits, can fly a high-powered jet, and saves her husband. Once her daughter gains some self-confidence, she also shows some very effective powers and saves the family on more than one occasion.

A female character also saves the day in *Wall-E*, when robot Eve repairs the title character after he is damaged trying to help the humans in the film return to Earth.

In *A Bug's Life*, the focus of the film is a colony of ants. As in real life, the ants are led by a queen, but male and female characters contribute equally to the story and to the rescue of the colony. The queen's daughter, Princess Atta, even manages to help lead male Flick escape certain death and, together, they see that the bad guy is taken care of.

These films are all popular with children, making it clear that having female characters in strong roles does not hurt the bottom line. Yet they remain more of an exception than a rule: kids' films still feature nearly all-male casts with females in minor roles, if they are present at all.

On television, it is more of the same—the shows that appeal most to boys or mixed audiences are anchored by male characters:

- SpongeBob, Patrick, Squidward, and Mr. Krabs from *SpongeBob SquarePants.*
- King Julien, Mort, Maurice, and the entire team of penguins from *Penguins of Madagascar.*
- Johnny from *Johnny Test.*
- Timmy from *Fairly Odd Parents.*
- Otis from *Back at the Barnyard.*
- Phineas and Ferb, the stars of their eponymous show.
- Ben Tennyson in *Ben 10: Alien Force.*
- Dan from the *Bakugan* series.
- Iron Man, Hulk, Thor, Wolverine, Silver Surfer, and Captain America from *Super Hero Squad.*
- Spider-Man and Batman, stars of their own series.

In fact, it is exceedingly difficult to find any female-led shows for young boys. In the roster of programs on Canadian channel Teletoon, there are but two shows anchored by female characters—*Atomic Betty* and *Totally Spies.* The former is a good show, albeit with some stereotyped high-school-aged characters. The latter is an action show that features three tall, thin teenage girls who talk like Valley Girls, get screechy over dirt and slime, and have a male "boss" (à la Charlie's Angels) who gives them gadgets like a "multi-function charm bracelet, net-throwing extendable rod mascara, [and] inflatable lint roller."[7] *Totally Spies* draws an audience consisting equally of male and female viewers[8] and while it is good to see an action show led by females who possess bravery and some degree of intelligence, it is unfortunate that the characters are so highly stereotyped. Some aspects of the show may be tongue-in-cheek (like the gadgets), but stereotypes still prevail.

In TV series with an ensemble of male and female characters, the males tend to dominate. The "face" of the three *Bakugan Battle Brawlers* series is Dan. Over on *Pokemon*, it is Ash. There is one girl among the main characters (at least the human ones) on *Hot Wheels Battle Force 5* and *Chaotic*. Superhero shows that focus on a collective of heroes—like *Justice League* and *Wolverine and the X-Men*—involve females to a great degree but often position the males as more prominent. This is especially true of the animated series *Super Hero Squad*.

Super Hero Squad is ostensibly about the many heroes in the Marvel Comics universe. There is a core team that is aided at various times by other heroes. Female characters like Storm, Black Widow, and Songbird make guest appearances but the main cast is almost entirely male. The lone female listed as a feature character on the show's website is Ms. Marvel, but she is really a bit player.

In the first episode of the series Ms. Marvel is shown defending Super Hero City against marauding monsters, but in subsequent episodes she is much less involved. In one plotline, she is even excluded when the males go out for a night on the town, having been assigned the menial task of counting paper clips on the team's HeliCarrier, much to the amusement of Iron Man.[9] Her secondary role with the team is made obvious in other ways—she is referred to sarcastically as "Mom," nicknamed "Ms. Crankypants," and told by male character Falcon that she is not his boss, just his landlady.[10]

Despite some highly negative female portrayals, all is not lost in the world of television. With so many males, it is hard for females to carve out a niche as strong or heroic characters but a few have managed to do just that.

While not showing girls as heroic in the traditional sense of the word, there are a couple of programs that show females as problem solvers. *Grossology* has a brother/sister duo as leads and both are smart, competent investigators. Similarly, the classic *Scooby-Doo, Where Are You* and *The Scooby-Doo Show* involve both male and female characters in the solutions to the shows' mysteries.

The live-action series *Power Rangers: RPM* is dominated by men but makes the most of its female characters. The mysterious Dr. K, seen only as a machine in the first few episodes and assumed to be a man, is later revealed to be a woman. She is the inventor of the Power Rangers and the technologies that keep the city safe. It is often Dr. K who saves the day with new gizmos and power sources for the Rangers. Yes, she could be considered a stereotypical nerd, but females with an affinity for science are rare in kids' TV and Dr. K provides a good example for both boys and girls to see.

Summer is the lone female Power Ranger but she possesses skills equivalent to the males. Because the Power Rangers need contributions from the whole team to be successful, she plays an integral role in all of the fights. Her backstory is a bit stereotypical—she was a spoiled heiress until crisis forced her to change her ways—but she is an equal member of the team and treated as such by the other Rangers. Unfortunately, the highly stereotyped male characters on this series undermine its attempts at gender balance.

Gwen Tennyson, cousin of Ben on *Ben 10: Alien Force*, is also a strong and capable character. She is calm and collected in the face of danger and routinely shows that she can take care of her own safety and that of the people around her, including Ben. Agura from *Hot Wheels Battle Force 5* is another strong female who is a valued part of her team, as is the sentient computer known as Sage.

Gwen, Agura, Summer, and Dr. K are strong exceptions to the no-female-hero rule, but their ability to influence girls outside of their television programs (which are predominantly marketed to boys) is minimal. None of them appear in toys marketed to girls. In fact, few toys that include an element of rescue in their intended use—like fire fighter or police costumes or superhero toys—are targeted to girls.

Looking in the 2009 Toys R Us Christmas catalogue, the so-called girls' toys include the usual assortment of feminine things—baby dolls, vanities, make-up, Barbies, and princesses—but there is not a single toy aimed at girls that allows them the fantasy of rescuing or being heroic in some fashion (unless you count the act of parenting which, in the real world, does require a lot of strength and stamina).

Beyond taking care of baby, girls reading this Toys R Us catalogue are encouraged do little more than dress up and look pretty. There are no images of girls as paramedics, fire fighters, or doctors, even though boys are shown in those roles. The closest girls can get to the medical profession is being a "pet doctor" like Barbie. (Note the absence of the more scientific term "veterinarian.") Checking the Toys R Us website a few months later, there appears to have been some progress. After three pages of princess and fairy costumes, the Girls' Pretend Play section shows a veterinarian's costume, a doctor's costume, and a train conductor's costume. There are still no rescue hero costumes, but at least there is something other than the pink and frilly fare usually made available to girls.[11]

Toys R Us is not the only toy vendor to fall prey to stereotypes. Both online and in its print catalogues, Canadian retailer Chapters/Indigo tells shoppers that rescue toys are more suited to boys. On the company's website, toys for children aged 5 to 8 years can be filtered by gender. Boys' toys include a lot of knights and pirates, along with fire trucks and, interestingly, a dress-up cloak called an "adventure cape." Girls' toys include a wide selection of options for dressing up as fairies, princesses, ballerinas, or witches, but no fire trucks and no adventure capes.[12]

Toy vendors may not be entirely culpable. They could very well be responding to a market that prefers toys segregated by gender. For their part, parents are not bound by what toy vendors tell them—they can buy fire trucks for their daughters and baby dolls for their sons. Girls who like princess costumes can easily imagine themselves as dragon slayers and not passive girls awaiting rescue. But the gender stereotypes that are present in toy marketing are powerful and exert an equally strong influence on children of both sexes, reinforcing the lessons already taught by television and film—boys and men do the important, demanding, and heroic work while girls and women cook, clean, and obsess over looking pretty.

This message is repeated in the world of video games. The very popular *New Super Mario Brothers* video game includes a female, but relegates her to a passive role. "Poor" Princess Peach, ostensibly the ruler of the kingdom, gets kidnapped and it is up to Mario, his brother Luigi, and two Toad characters (gender unknown) to rescue her. The object of *Mario & Luigi Bowser's Inside Story* is similar. Mario, Luigi, and Peach all get swallowed by the villainous Bowser, but only Mario and Luigi see any action as they attempt to save the princess.

In the literary world, the situation is not quite so dire. Some books include gender-typical depictions of adults: in *Mudshark,* the school secretary, nurse, cook, and librarian are female, while the custodian and principal are male; *Captain Underpants* also features a female secretary and male principal; a male principal runs the school in the *Horrible Harry* series; and the *Barnes and the Brains* series includes a male science teacher and a female librarian. But there are plenty of books that show girls as intelligent, inquisitive, and capable of working productively with boys. The *Magic Tree House* and *Judy Moody* series are two examples, as are the books of Robert Munsch.

In the case of books, it is not so much a lack of balanced materials, but a focus on pushing boys away from them that is the problem.

The issue of boys' literacy is a sensitive one. For years now, studies from around the world have shown that boys' literacy scores are significantly lower than girls'. To combat this decline, there is a trend in classrooms and parenting guides to direct reluctant male readers towards genres and formats that boys tend to like: non-fiction, magazines, series, stories with humour, science fiction, and fantasy. Yet, if we are to believe the creators of recommended reading lists for boys, books that feature girls are not relevant to male children.

Recommended reading lists for boys from various public libraries and the *Guys Read* site (created by children's book author Jon Scieszka) are dominated by books with male protagonists—*Stuart Little* but no *Charlotte's Web*, *Encyclopedia Brown* but no *Judy Moody*, Abe Lincoln but no Amelia Earheart. (Interestingly, Earheart's story is included in Scieszka's *Time Warp Trio* series, but her story does not rate a mention in the list of books he recommends for boys.)

I do not question the quality of many of the recommended books, but I do question the strategy. Jump starting boys' interest in reading with books about male characters may be a great idea initially, but at some point boys need to be taught to value stories in general, not just stories about boys.

There are excellent series that feature females in non-traditional roles or male/female duos as protagonists, but many boys will miss out because they are directed instead to books that focus on males and the things they are supposedly interested in. According to *Guys Read*, this list of interests includes: monkeys and/or apes; sports; at least one explosion; war; outer space with aliens; boxers, wrestlers and ultimate fighters; and ghosts.[13]

While there is no denying that certain topics appeal more to boys, these recommended book lists do not give fictional girls a chance, nor do they provide options for boys whose interests might fall outside of apes, fighting, and blowing things up.

By having their scope of interest narrowed, even with the best of intentions, boys will continue to believe that stories about women and girls are less interesting and less relevant to them, simply because they are about the opposite sex. They will also come face to face with yet another source of male stereotypes, which begs the question, are these lists helping boys or hurting them? Is it beneficial to boys in the long run to give them reading materials that promote such hoary male stereotypes as the superhero or ultimate fighter, the smart-alecky underachiever, and the bratty practical joker? And is it right to assume that a young boy would not be interested in a story about a smart protagonist who collects dead moths, band-aids, and toothpicks if this protagonist were a girl?[14] (Which in this case, she is.) I, for one, have my doubts.

Boys need a full range of options in their book lists to keep them interested in reading. Books about girls should be part of this mix. While princess and fairy stories may not resonate with boys, books with females doing typical kid stuff, or non-fiction books about women— like the aforementioned Earheart, astronaut Roberta Bondar, or hockey player Hayley Wickenheiser—would certainly find some fans among male readers.

Creating Balance and Promoting Gender Equality

It might be assumed that the consequences of male dominance in children's entertainment are more severe for girls, who see their own sex drastically under-represented, but boys suffer as well.

The idea of male dominance is an insidious one. Although it may not show any effects in a boy as young as seven or eight, it could have ramifications as that boy ages, especially if there is no counterbalance in his daily life.

Gender imbalance in pop culture teaches boys that men are more important than girls and that males should set the agenda, whether in the domestic setting or the workplace. This imbalance is evidence of William Pollack's big wheel imperative, mentioned in Chapter 1, which describes the pressure men feel to achieve status and power.

As Pollack notes, the notion that males are natural leaders or authority figures places stress on boys and men, making them feel that they need to perform at their highest level at all times. It also teaches boys to maintain a façade of control, even when things are not going as planned, while never giving into feelings of doubt or betraying the slightest hint of weakness.[15]

Boys who consider men more important than women may also develop a sense of entitlement that leaves them ill-prepared for a society in which females play a far more significant role than pop culture has led them to believe. Although men still dominate many areas of the real world, women make important contributions in a variety of ways. Boys who grow up without a realistic view of women's skills and accomplishments may experience diminished self-esteem or loss of confidence when they realize that their sex, which may open doors, does not guarantee them higher status or more prestige than their female peers.

Including more female characters in boys' entertainment would counter the negative impact of male dominance and teach boys to see men and women as equals. Of course, these female characters cannot be token love interests. They must be strong, smart, independent, and capable, just like the boys.

Chapter 5: Modern Day Warriors: Superheroes and Sports Stars

In June of 1938, Action Comics #1 introduced a new comic book series that was, in the words of co-creator Jerry Siegel, "something that was very different. Something that the public would really take to its heart."[1] The series chronicled the life of a new kind of hero who was quite unlike his counterparts in the adventure strips of the day, Buck Rogers and Tarzan among them. That new character—faster than a speeding bullet and able to leap tall buildings in a single bound—was Superman.

The Man of Steel and the many caped crusaders who followed him have indeed been taken to heart, especially by young boys. The current big four in the superhero genre—Spider-Man, Batman, Wolverine, and, to a lesser extent these days, Superman—have all spawned multiple films and television series. New animated television series featuring Iron Man have added yet another hero to current kids' popular culture, and upcoming feature films (and the merchandise tie-ins sure to accompany them) will introduce Green Lantern and Captain America to an entirely new generation of boys.

What makes superheroes so attractive to young boys? According to Ellen Jordan, nobody knows: "We have, as far as I know, little in the way of explanation of how or why these narratives gain such a grip on little boys, but evidence that they do, and have done for generations, is inescapable."[2]

I would guess that the potent combination of fearlessness, physical strength, and the desire to do good deeds is behind the popularity of superheroes. There's also the cool factor attached to each hero's trademark crime-fighting tools: Batman's gadgets, Wolverine's claws, Spider-Man's webs, and Superman's panoply of powers.

Whatever the reason, most young boys (and some girls—myself included) fall under the spell of a superhero at one time or another.

Added into this mix is a different kind of hero who is also considered super by many young boys. The professional athlete—especially in marquee sports like hockey, football, baseball, and basketball—has long captured the imagination of young boys, who proudly wear jerseys and T-shirts emblazoned with his number, collect trading cards with his image, and buy the equipment he endorses.

And what are boys learning from these heroes, fictional or real? Certainly, the lessons are not all bad, but neither are they all good.

Speak Softly and Carry a Big Stick

When most people think of superheroes, they think of physical feats of daring. Being superhuman, these heroes are shown doing things that the average person cannot. And while some may speak softly about the need for peace, superheroes are routinely thrust into situations that call for the proverbial big stick.

The violence that heroes use is just one troubling aspect of the superhero genre. Through their actions and attitudes, superheroes exhibit many of the traits associated with traditional masculinity: reliance on physical strength and dominance, aggression, and a lack of physical and emotional vulnerability. In some superhero narratives, there are also indications that male heroes have more to offer than females.

As much as they reinforce stereotypes, superheroes are not without their virtues. These characters have good intentions and are willing to devote themselves to helping humankind, sacrificing any chance they might have at a so-called normal life. They have strong morals and always choose right over wrong. According to Penny Holland, Academic Leader for Early Childhood Studies at London Metropolitan University and author of *We don't play with guns here*, there are additional benefits in the "good versus evil" narrative that superhero stories typically follow.

In her book, Holland explores the impact of relaxing the zero-tolerance approach to war, weapon, and superhero play that prevails in UK child care centres. She argues that strict bans on this type of play (which I will abbreviate to "warrior play") should be reconsidered and she offers plenty of reasons why.

Warrior play can help children deal with the violent and aggressive behaviour they see on TV, in movies, on the playground, and even at home. As Holland notes, instead of ignoring the violent images children encounter, adults can give children the chance to "process and imaginatively transform such material" through pretend play based on their favourite warrior characters, including heroes like Spider-Man, Batman, and Superman.

And, contrary to what most adults think, this kind of play does not lead to an increase in aggressive behaviour. Research has shown that only about 1% of pretend play leads to real aggression, although the numbers rise among children who already have aggressive tendencies. As psychologist Jerome Singer states in reference to toy soldier sets:

such toys can be conducive to generating imaginative play without provoking overtly violent behaviour ... It could be argued that one reason some children act out aggressive behaviour directly (in addition to imitating the adult violence they may experience in the family or vicariously) is that ... they have not practised, starting with pretend play, their capacity to play out possibilities in a miniaturized mental world, and by so doing learned to explore negative as well as positive consequences of linking direct actions to wishes and emotions.[3]

For children who are at risk of anti-social or aggressive behaviour, warrior play provides an outlet with positive outcomes—engagement in the play group and the chance to exercise their creative muscle through imaginative play. Even for kids who are not considered "at risk," warrior play offers equal benefits in imaginative development. When kids pretend they talk more, they share and resolve conflict, they uncover common interests with others, and they build friendships.

While all kinds of imaginative play can have these positive effects, only warrior play tends to be frowned upon or even banned by adults. For some kids (usually boys), this is a big problem because warrior play can be "the spark that ignites [their] interest" in pretend play.

Being in favour of superhero and similar types of play does not mean supporting the kind of fighting that superheroes tend to employ. Rather, it means giving children the freedom to explore solutions to the problems they encounter in everyday life, like how to handle the bad guy or process anger.

By emulating their heroes, boys can develop the confidence to tackle problems and learn to support each other in their efforts to face down threats and fears, whether real or imagined. For that reason, war, weapon and superhero play can be a very good thing. But superheroes, especially as they are depicted on current television programs, can have a detrimental effect on a boy's understanding of masculinity and femininity.

Let's begin with the idea that heroics are the domain of men. I discussed the general preference for male heroes in the previous chapter, but it is also apparent in the world of superheroes. Female superheroes, while making strides, have not yet achieved the stature of the males. What's worse, their achievements are often diminished by their curvaceous, scantily-clad bodies and occasional objectification by male characters.

The seven-member Justice League includes two women—Wonder Woman and Hawkgirl. Both are strong heroes and presented as equal to the men. The League members work as a team and the women are a valuable part of their efforts. Like the Justice League, the X-Men have seven principal characters, including three women who are involved in the plot and shown as capable and heroic. *Super Hero Squad* is another animated series that includes female heroes. These female characters are welcome additions to the superhero genre, but there are signs that they are not quite in the same "league" as the men.

The first clue is their appearance. As in many animated programs, the women are highly sexualized. All of the women in the X-Men have doe eyes, large breasts, and tiny waists. Many, like Emma Frost, wear extremely revealing outfits. The women in *Super Hero Squad* are very muscular but also have large breasts and, in some cases, wear questionable outfits. (Screaming Mimi and Storm are two examples.) In the Justice League, Wonder Woman and Hawkgirl wear what appear to be strapless bathing suits. In contrast, the men, while excessively muscular, are at least fully clothed.

The female heroes on these programs also have full lips and long, flowing hair, a hallmark of femininity which, while meant to signal attractiveness, seems a little impractical for women who routinely engage in physical battles against a wide assortment of enemies.

Women, whether heroes or not, are also objectified to a far greater degree than men: Emma Frost is looked up and down by Angel when she first appears in *Wolverine and the X-Men*. Thief Gambit notes the beauty of his client Zane on another episode of the same show. Booster Gold hits on the "beautiful" scientist he rescues in an episode of *Justice League*, referring to her as a "damsel in distress" and a "hot doctor." The League is also the home of Flash, who is regularly shown making moves on women. Over on *Super Hero Squad*, all of the men gush over Black Widow, and Iron Man tells the evil Enchantress that "even in defeat you're a striking woman. What's say you and I have a little dinner."[4]

The fact that many of these women are assigned powers that are less physically demanding than those of the men also implies that they are less traditionally heroic than their male counterparts. The *Justice League* version of Wonder Woman is a notable exception—while she does not possess super speed, she can fly and appears to be nearly as strong as Superman. (These traits are absent from the *Super Friends* version of Wonder Woman.) Hawkgirl can also fly and is a formidable fighter, but the other female heroes with whom today's boys are acquainted tend to have powers of the mind, like telekinesis and telepathy (Jean Grey and Emma Frost), the ability to control weather (Storm), or the ability to phase through things (Shadowcat).

All are great attributes, to be sure, but they do not compare to the brute force of the men. Nor are the women's powers likely to appeal to boys' imaginations as much as Flash's super speed, Superman's x-ray and heat vision, Spider-Man's web slinging, or Wolverine's ability to slice through any substance on Earth with adamantium claws.

In the world of professional sports, men are also shown as stronger and faster, mainly because female athletes are rarely featured or even mentioned in sports broadcasts.

According to research by Children Now, some 90% of American boys between the ages of 8 and 17 watch televised sports.[5] Numbers for Canada were not available but they would likely be similar, and might even skew younger given anecdotal evidence I have gathered of boys in the primary grades watching hockey, baseball, and football. Given that action figures based on Ultimate Fighting Championship (UFC) stars are being promoted to boys aged six and up,[6] it is reasonable to assume that some young males have had exposure to this extremely violent "sport" as well.

And what are boys seeing in the televised sports they watch? Male players, male coaches, and, for the most part, male announcers, although female reporters have made some progress in the field of sports broadcasting. Most sports news programs include a woman on the anchor desk. In sports like professional football, women are present, albeit with minor roles as sideline reporters. NBA broadcasts have included female basketball stars as sideline reporters and in-booth analysts. *Hockey Night in Canada* has added hockey star Cassie Campbell to its lineup and even allowed her a role as colour commentator. American women's hockey star Cammi Granato has had a similar role in the United States, but in most sports, it is all men all the time.

Major League Baseball (MLB) is one example. MLB Network, which covers MLB games and news, has a few female reporters but no women in the broadcast booth.[7] A similar situation exists for my hometown Toronto Blue Jays, who have no women in the booth or on the field.

(As a side note, I will point out that a Google search for "female sports broadcasters" demonstrates where these women rank in the minds of some male viewers. Among the entries that appear are "25 Sexiest Female Sports Broadcasters," "Most Attractive Female Sports Broadcasters—NFL," "Who is the hottest female sports personality in Canada," and "World's Hottest Female Sports Reporters." No such entries resulted from a search for "male sports broadcasters.")

A 2009 article in the *Journal of Sport Behavior* discusses the role of the media in perpetuating the idea that sports are the domain of men. The study's authors asked college students to rate various sports on a scale of "hyper masculine" to "hyper feminine," then examined how participants' attitudes were affected by sports participation, gender socialization, and media consumption.

Their conclusion, while limited by the small sample size, was that "sports continue to be conceptualized as a generally masculine endeavour with the exception of a few activities." These "feminine" activities include non-aggressive sports like volleyball and gymnastics.

By examining the influences in people's lives, this study also demonstrates that views on gender (traditional or otherwise) and a person's own experience playing sports have no impact on their attitudes about the gender appropriateness of a sport. The greatest influence on people's views is the "televised sports manhood formula"—the repeated images of men participating in sports. The more people see men playing certain sports, the more they associate these activities with the male sex. Attitudes could very well change, the authors note, by including more females in sports broadcasts.[8]

How skewed are sports broadcasts? A 2010 study done by USC sociologist Mike Messner and Purdue sociologist Cheryl Cooky found that stories about male athletes occupied 96% of sports news stories on network news and ESPN Sportscenter in 2009. Not only were men featured more prominently, but coverage of women's sports had actually dropped from 6.3% of stories on network affiliates in 2004 to just 1.6% in 2009. As the study's authors note, this discrepancy is important because "it reinforces the historical stereotype that sports prove men are superior to women, [and] that the women's product isn't the same quality or would not have the same mass appeal."[9]

An article by Messner that appeared in *The Huffington Post* outlines the broader implications of this "televised sports manhood formula." Sports broadcasts and news shows do more than build an audience for men's sports, although they do that very effectively. They also, in Messner's words:

> tell us stories about who we are and promote values that are important to our understanding of women's and men's roles in families and public life. In the not too distant past, the story that sports told was that men were naturally superior to women, and were thus destined to dominate in politics, religion and medicine.

> The producers and editors (nearly all male) of TV sports news and highlights shows are helping to keep this outdated story alive by virtually ignoring women's sports.[10]

Beyond stereotyping women as less important than men, sports broadcasts also reinforce male stereotypes that place value on toughness and physical dominance.

On hockey telecasts, the emphasis on toughness is hard to avoid given the NHL's stubborn refusal to abolish fighting. Even baseball is known to have the occasional bench-clearing brawl, with some observers praising the players for having "moxie" or "fire."[11]

In the play-by-play and colour commentary heard during many games it is the norm for players to be described in terms of their physical attributes (especially in football). "Tough" seems to be one of the most commonly used terms, and height and weight statistics are routinely trotted out to emphasize how powerful a player is.

If a player is smaller than average, descriptions of his accomplishments are often prefaced with a comment like "despite his size," as though a smaller man is immediately assumed to be weaker or less competent. A prime example is quarterback Doug Flutie who, in the words of one-time Toronto Argonaut teammate Mike "Pinball" Clemons, was "[d]espite being productive ... mentioned more for his lack of size than his tremendous skill."[12] Flutie later went on to join the National Football League (NFL), whose teams had once passed him over because of his small stature.

Other headlines make reference to the small size of male athletes. NFL cornerback Mark McMillian was once said in *The Sporting News* to "thrive despite lack of ideal size."[13] A 2010 profile notes that a college football player "piques NFL interest despite his size."[14] An Ontario Hockey League player was recognized for protecting the puck well "despite his size."[15] Another junior hockey player's size was referenced multiple times in one article. Carlos Amestoy was referred to on the *HockeyNow* website as being of "small stature," "diminutive," "just 5-7" and "only" weighing 155 pounds—a player who "despite his size" hoped to have a big impact on his next team. While his skill is noted, the article also states that Amestoy was trying to put on weight.[16]

Hockey and football are very physical, violent sports and sportswriters may have legitimate concerns that a man who is 5'7" might not fare well against opponents who are typically much larger. Still, it is interesting that men who are of smaller stature and have the statistics to back up their athletic accomplishments face judgments that male athletes of ideal size do not. What message is this sending to young boys? On the one hand, they see a man succeed despite the odds, but on the other, they see clear evidence that people in our society prejudge smaller men, assuming that they are inherently less capable than bigger men.

An emphasis on physical power is not the only negative aspect of televised sports. A study by the organization Children Now explores some of the messages delivered by professional sports, as presented in the popular media. Among them are the ideas that aggression is rewarded and that playing with pain is heroic. Most televised sports also promote violence through regular replays of hits and fights and the use of martial language (arsenal, battle, blitz, reloading, shotgun) to describe games and some of the plays within them.[17]

All told, the images presented by superheroes and sports broadcasts contribute to the idea that heroes are tough, aggressive, and male. Of course, to be tough, these men must be physically strong. Boys watching fictional superheroes and real-world sports stars quickly learn that the ideal male is tall and muscular, with hulking biceps and six-pack abs.

This message is not a new one. Since the 1940s and 1950s, the era of Muscle Beach and Charles Atlas, young men have aspired to a more muscular physique. That trend has continued, but the age at which body dissatisfaction first occurs has decreased and the tendency to opt for steroids and growth hormones to achieve a perfect body has increased.

Recent research has shown that boys as young as 8 struggle with body image, 25% of boys between the ages of 10 and 14 are dieting to lose weight,[18] and 41% of boys aged 13 to 19 are dissatisfied with their bodies. The authors of *The Adonis Complex* found that, when given a choice between body types, more than half of boys aged 11 to 17 preferred a figure that possessed about 35 pounds more muscle than they possessed themselves—an ideal that for most males can only be attained by using steroids.[19] This desire for huge muscles would explain why some boys begin experimenting during adolescence with protein supplements and steroids to increase their muscle mass. According to the organization Common Sense Media, one-third of teenage boys even resort to laxatives and smoking to help control their weight.[20]

Unlike the case for females, who generally want to be smaller, there are two extremes in male body dissatisfaction, with some boys concerned that they are too big and others worried that they are not big enough. Studies from the United States, Great Britain, and Australia routinely find that about 25% of prepubescent boys want to be thinner,[21] while other research has shown that concern about muscularity also begins before puberty.[22]

Where does body dissatisfaction originate? Books like *The Lolita Effect* and studies like *Eating Disorders and the Role of the Media*[23] have drawn clear links between the media and body image issues for girls. Researchers who study body image and boys note that while a variety of influences contribute to body dissatisfaction—including parents and peers—"the lean but muscular male ideal increasingly portrayed in advertising and other media may be as harmful for men as thin ideals are for women."[24] They have also noted that many of the earliest messages a child receives about the ideal body come from television, movies, and toys.[25]

A 2005 study called "Action Figures and Men," which appeared in the journal *Sex Roles*, investigated whether playing with action figures lowered the body esteem of participants. This study used adults and the researchers cautioned that results were preliminary, but there was evidence of a significant impact on body esteem: the more muscular the figure, the worse participants felt about their own bodies.[26] The results of this study cannot be applied directly to boys, but it is not much of a leap to assume that adult perceptions of the ideal male body type have their origins in over-muscled childhood heroes.

As for TV and film, in their book *The psychology of men's health*, health psychology professors Christina Lee and R. Glynn Owens[27] argue that exposure to stereotyped media images of "attractive men as large and muscular" raises boys' awareness of "the social value placed on muscle bulk."

Lee and Owens believe that "[g]endered expectations that men should be large and muscular affect the self-esteem of all men, and some groups ... experience severe distress and dysfunctional behaviour as a result." Further, they argue "for a broader recognition of the insidious effects that gender role expectations may have in this as in other areas of life, and for a more fundamental challenging of these role expectations, such that the individual can learn to reject these and instead to accept himself on his own terms."[28]

Superheroes, as the epitome of masculinity, shoulder at least some of the blame for boys' body image problems. Whether flying through the sky, swinging on a web between skyscrapers, or tackling a criminal to the ground, their physical feats take precedence over any other attributes they may possess. Carrying out such heroic exploits requires a certain physique that was evident in the muscular superheroes of my childhood, but has reached new extremes in today's animated heroes. The ideal body is exemplified by the men of the Justice League who have hulking chests, chiselled biceps, and small waists. Wolverine takes this physique to an entirely new level with his disproportionately huge chest and biceps. The Hulk, sometime colleague of Wolverine, is a monster of a man and even the comparatively smaller Spider-Man has perfect musculature, evident in his tights, but not apparent in his alter-ego, the "geeky" Peter Parker.

This discrepancy between Peter Parker and Spider-Man demonstrates the concept of metamorphosis, which juxtaposes the two extremes of the male experience—the muscular hero and the "nerdy" everyman.

The idea of metamorphosis is common in films aimed at girls. A 2008 study of princess movies shows that in more than two-thirds of these films, the female leads are "put on exhibition" through a royal engagement, a wedding, or a skill-based activity. Most are evaluated solely for their appearance and if they aren't up to snuff, they undergo "an extreme makeover." The classic example of metamorphosis is, of course, Cinderella being transformed by her fairy godmother.[29]

The same kind of transformation occurs with male superheroes and, while these changes are excused because they all have secret identities to maintain, the end result is equally stereotypical.

Passive Peter Parker is called a nerd and a geek in the animated series *Spectacular Spider-Man*. As such, he cannot fight crime as he is—he must transform himself into a muscle-bound, wall-crawling, web-slinging hero. In the cartoon series *Iron Man: Armored Adventures*, Tony Stark, described by his friend as "an absent-minded, dorky kid," becomes "a different person" when he puts on his armour.[30] In the superhero-like *Ben 10:Alien Force*, Ben Tennyson morphs from an average teenage boy to any one of ten alien heroes, some of whom are truly gigantic. All of these characters take their cues from the original nerd/hero—clumsy Clark Kent who undergoes a radical change every time he steps into a phone booth, entering in glasses and conservative clothing and emerging as Superman in tights that emphasize his perfect male figure.

Many boys may draw inspiration from the compelling narrative of an unassuming or bullied kid being transformed into a larger-than-life hero. And while it is wonderful to teach boys that they have the potential to be a hero despite the sometimes harsh judgments of others, superheroes also teach boys another, less positive lesson—strength of character is nice to have, but it will never win the day. To be a true hero, a man must be physically strong and visibly muscular.

The increasing importance of rippling muscles was first seen in the 1980s with the rise of "steroid-stoked bodies" in popular films[31] and is evident in today's super-sized superheroes. A comparison of images from the 1970s series *Super Friends* and today's *Justice League* shows how much these characters have grown. Today's incarnations of Superman and Batman are significantly larger in the chest and shoulders than the older versions, with one author claiming that Batman's shoulders have "morphed from one-fourth of his height to almost half of his height."[32] Even B-list *Justice League* hero Aquaman has changed from a fit and defined half-man/half-fish to a hulking Neptune-like character with gigantic biceps.

In the past 25 years, action figures have also bulked up. While not a superhero in the conventional sense, G.I. Joe is a popular male action figure whose 1964 version, when translated into human terms, had a 44-inch chest and 12-inch biceps. By the mid-1990s, Joe's chest had expanded to 55 inches and his biceps to a highly unrealistic 27.2 inches.[33] One version of the Wolverine action figure, when translated to a man 5 feet 10 inches tall, would have a biceps measurement of 32 inches—just one inch less than his waist. Even action figures for Luke Skywalker and Han Solo of *Star Wars* fame beefed up considerably in the seventeen years between the film's original release and its re-release.[34] My son's superhero action figures, with waist measurements half the size of their chests, promote the same, virtually unattainable silhouette. Newer action figures based on WWE wrestlers and UFC mixed martial arts fighters have similar proportions.

Physiques like these put action figures into or beyond body builder range—not exactly the average man. By way of comparison, bodybuilder Steve Reeves—a man who was considered to have had the most perfectly proportioned (and drug-free) body ever—had a chest measurement of 52 inches, a waist of 29 inches, and a biceps measurement of 18.25 inches.[35] Even wrestler Hulk Hogan, who has admitted to steroid use,[36] has a biceps measurement of 24 inches—a full 3.2 inches less than G.I. Joe and 8 inches less than Wolverine.[37]

There are definite parallels between today's outsize action figures and that lightning rod for feminist ire, Barbie. Barbie is often criticized for her extreme proportions. In human dimensions, she would be 5'9", weigh 110 pounds, and have measurements of 36-18-33.[38] Clearly, current male action figures are just as guilty as Barbie of promoting a completely unrealistic body ideal.

The danger of exposing young boys to such extreme body images is, according to *The Adonis Complex*, that children are not old enough to stop and question whether the level of muscularity in their favourite action heroes is realistic or even a reasonable goal for a man's body.

This constant, distorted messaging about the ideal male body, present in boys' lives from preschool age through the adult years, can have a considerable negative impact. Body image is very closely tied to self-esteem in boys, especially among those who are short or late developing. In fact, appearance is more important for most teenage boys than academic or athletic achievement or even acceptance by their friends. Some studies have also shown that boys with a negative body image are more prone to depression.

Adding to the problem for boys is that most parents are unaware of body image problems in their sons. They may be attuned to similar problems in their daughters, but many assume that body dissatisfaction does not affect boys. Cultural imperatives dictating that boys should not talk about their concerns exacerbate the problem. As boys get older, they often internalize their worries about their bodies and, "in the absence of feedback from their families...listen to other voices," including television and other pop culture outlets that perpetuate the over-muscled masculine ideal.[39]

Beyond the physical, there is an emotional aspect to the lives of superheroes that troubles some observers. Child psychologists Dan Kindlon and Michael Thompson, authors of *Raising Cain*, note that in superhero comic books and the movies and TV shows based on them, the idea of isolation is often romanticized. Superman disappears to his Fortress of Solitude. Batman finds solace in the BatCave. Wolverine takes off on his motorcycle whenever the mood moves him. None of these men talk about what is troubling them—they just withdraw.

Superhero narratives that focus on isolation reflect traditional views of masculinity, which dictate that "a man should be strong, silent and self-contained" and that he should not express his emotions or ask for help when he is troubled. Male denial of emotional needs and lack of emotional expression are entirely socially constructed—there is no biological reason behind them.[40] Yet, many young boys are brought up believing that their sex precludes emotional openness. And when emotional expression is frowned upon, withdrawal may seem to be the only option.

The danger of withdrawal is that boys unwittingly deny themselves a chance to resolve the problems they are facing. Failure to deal with problems can lead to stress and tension and, in extreme cases, depression.[41]

Boys' lack of emotional expression is a very complex issue. Cultural imperatives toward stoicism in men are, admittedly, just one part of the problem, but teaching boys to view talking and emotional expression as positive actions could go a long way toward helping them negotiate the difficulties they face as they grow up.

Fortunately, the creators of most superhero programs aimed at children have gotten the message. The theme of isolation may have been common in superhero stories at one time but it is less prevalent now, save for one notable exception. Newer animated versions of superhero stories show the heroes with close friends: Tony Stark (Iron Man) has Pepper and Rhodey to talk to; Peter Parker has many good friends (although none know his secret); Ben Tennyson of *Ben 10* has his cousin Gwen, his girlfriend Julie, and his former nemesis, Kevin; and shows like *Justice League* and *Super Hero Squad* highlight teamwork.

Even Wolverine, a classic loner, is shown to be something of a team player on *Wolverine and the X-Men*. Comments by his colleagues initially depict him as someone who never asks for help and has a tendency to disappear—a "leader who's never there."[42] But Wolverine takes their words to heart, reunites the disparate elements of the X-Men team, and assumes the role of leader.

Still, the concept of the brooding hero has not been completely erased, thanks to Batman. In *Justice League* and *Justice League Unlimited* storylines, Batman is presented as a moody, shadowy figure. It is rare for other League members to give him orders or cross him. He seems to be in his own world, almost set apart from the others and is, in fact, considered a "part-time" member of the League.[43]

Batman is evidence of the loner trope—a familiar one in popular culture. Characters that fill this role have an undeniable allure. As dark and tortured souls they create intrigue and draw people into a story. But for all of their appeal, they still reinforce the idea that emotional distance and isolation have value. For impressionable young boys, this may be a lesson that does more harm than good.

Although isolation and denial of emotions appear to be on the wane in many hero narratives, these stories are plagued by another kind of denial—that of physical vulnerability. Despite the extreme violence that characters in superhero shows endure, they never seem to sustain any injuries.

Fights are typically instigated by the bad guys, but heroes—even those who preach peace—are ultimately positioned as having no choice but to respond in kind when physically threatened by a villain. They have to fight fire with fire, and when they do, look out!

The violence in programs like *Justice League, Spectacular Spider-Man,* and *Wolverine and the X-Men* is excessive and gratuitous. It includes techniques like head butting, stomping, punches to the head, the occasional "clothesline," and martial arts style jumps and kicks. Characters are shown being spun around and thrown into walls. Images from the perspective of the victim add another disturbing element to the proceedings. In one chilling example from *Justice League,* the "camera" shifts quickly to Wonder Woman's viewpoint as a large man stomps on her head. Other programs show fists, feet, and kneecaps being slammed into characters' faces.

While it's true that "mild cartoon violence"—to use the words of today's ratings systems—has long been a part of animated superhero shows (and many others), the violence in current programs is relentless and far more graphic than in those of decades past. Current programs feature drawn-out, violent scenes in every episode, whereas older programs had long periods with no violence of any kind. In the first season of 1970s series *Super Friends,* stories were told over the course of several ten-minute episodes, some with not a hint of violence. In *Spider-Man,* which premiered in 1967, violence was also far less prevalent. In one episode, even the evil Dr. Octopus was immobilized simply and easily by a tangle of webs, without the web-slinging hero throwing a single punch.

Guns also make their presence felt in today's superhero shows. Large automatic weapons that shoot lasers and various other projectiles are commonplace, as are bombs of various kinds and fully armed helicopters. Some characters have weapons built-in, throwing firebombs with their hands or shooting lasers from their eyes.

As one can imagine, all this firepower causes untold destruction. It is not unusual for entire buildings to be destroyed during fights between heroes and villains. Schools, museums, shopping malls, parking garages, and warehouses are reduced to rubble in various episodes of these shows, often trapping a hero beneath the debris. Yet he or she always emerges, virtually unscathed, as do the "bad guys." (And the innocent bystanders? There is rarely any indication of their fate, although one episode of *Super Hero Squad* shows them being evacuated to shelters.)

The fact that superheroes are never gravely injured, despite being pummelled by a monstrous villain or crushed under a wall of bricks, teaches children that violence is a viable option for solving problems and that real heroes are invincible, or must at least appear so. Because the heroes are mostly male, the association between violence and masculinity is also made stronger.

The violence manifested in superhero cartoons has another effect. Boys who repeatedly see male heroes use force against their enemies are learning that anger is an acceptable reaction to being slighted. Granted, comic book foes are relentlessly evil so it is unrealistic to expect the hero to treat them with patience and kindness. Still, the lessons taught in the extreme worlds of Wolverine, Batman, and their superhero colleagues are easily transferable to the real world, especially by young boys who are learning how to deal with insults and seeking an appropriate response when someone upsets them. The same messages are delivered by athletes who react with anger or start fights.

While most boys have enough maturity and self-control to realize that they cannot hit a friend or sibling who has annoyed them, when they apply the lessons taught by their heroes, their initial reaction will be one of anger, not understanding. They may not hit, but they will feel insulted or wronged and tend to react accordingly, either by yelling, name calling, or using some kind of physical intimidation. Parents may help prevent the worst offenses by doling out discipline for inappropriate behaviour, but even that may not be enough to stop angry impulses from being acted upon.

Why do superhero programs contain so much violence? It seems that the creators of these and other children's action shows have assumed that violence appeals to boys, but does it really?

According to the International Central Institute for Youth and Educational Television (IZI) study *Girls and Boys and Television*, boys like action, insofar as it is used to master challenges. Violence and action are distinct entities for boys, and few actually seek out violent programming. Yet in most superhero shows and other programs aimed at boys, violence has become synonymous with action and is often used to resolve the challenges male characters face.[44]

The sports arena sends mixed signals on this issue. Players talk about sportsmanship and most practice it. But there are frequent examples of players taking it too far. The hockey world, where fights are a regular occurrence, has been rocked in recent years by some very violent hits, even in its junior leagues. Football has penalties for personal fouls, but outside of a loss of down and yardage, nothing is done about players who rough the quarterback, dole out late hits, or grab and twist another player's face mask. To their credit, most football commentators are quick to chastise players who do such things, but extremely rough play continues and is just as often excused as a sign of a player's intensity. The message to boys, as the Children Now study notes, is that aggression, even when taken too far, is okay or even laudable in the right circumstances.

Power Is Not Just Physical

Superheroes and athletes have a powerful hold on boys, of that there is no doubt. The impact of these heroes can be positive. With little more than a mask, if even that, a boy can pretend he is Batman. He can use his creativity to dream up new Bat-tools and envision himself saving the world. A boy with a hockey stick and a ball can picture himself as Sidney Crosby, scoring a winning goal. Tossing the football around with a friend, that same boy can imagine himself as Peyton Manning. In aspiring to be like their heroes, boys develop their imaginations, teach themselves about good and bad, and improve their self-esteem.

Unfortunately, there is a negative side to current hero narratives. From a young age, boys learn that acts of heroism are always physical—that they involve strength and, often, a good deal of violence (save for rescue heroes who, from what I have seen, lose their appeal after about age four when school starts and animated action heroes enter the picture). Heroism is rarely equated with peaceful solutions or thinking. This emphasis on the physical requires a certain body type—the kind that can dominate and vanquish the enemy. This body has rippling muscles, a tiny waist, and a barrel chest.

The overriding message in many sports is similar to what is communicated through superhero stories: toughness and aggression are the most valuable traits a male athlete possesses. The language used by commentators and the lack of female presence also contribute to the macho image of sports, again equating physical strength with masculinity.

Superheroes and professional sports are irresistible to most young boys and virtually impossible to excise from their lives. Because fictional heroes and athletes deliver some positive messages, there is no reason to eliminate them completely, but there is a need to talk about what boys see and hear in a superhero show or on a sports broadcast. (Suggestions for the content of these discussions can be found in Chapter 7).

During such talks, it is critical to tell young boys that: few men can achieve the body proportions of most athletes and superheroes; sportsmanship and non-violent solutions are always better than aggression; and women, whether real athletes or fictional heroes, can compete and achieve as much as men.

Chapter 6: Language and Communication

What is the first image that comes to mind when you read the word *catfight*? How about *nag, wimp,* or *wuss*?

Those terms undoubtedly conjure up images of two girls arguing, a sour-faced, critical woman, and a gawky boy overcome by fear or prone to excessive displays of emotion.

Note the gender specificity of those images: feline language, like *catfight*, would never be used to describe a disagreement between men, nor would a woman who shows signs of anxiety or emotional sensitivity ever be characterized as *wussy*.

Our language is filled with terms like these, whose negative overtones are inextricably linked to gender. That many of them make an appearance in children's popular culture is troubling because, in the words of sociolinguist Joan Swann, the gender imbalance expressed in this kind of language may, over time, "help to reinforce gender differences and inequalities [and] may influence children's perceptions of what are appropriate attributes, activities, occupations, and so forth for females and males."[1]

Gender perceptions are affected not only by what people say but by how they say it. Despite changes in gender roles in recent decades, our society still holds stereotyped assumptions about how men and women should sound. Because men are the "stronger sex," we expect that they will speak forcefully and in deep voices and that women, who are assumed to be more deferential, will use soft tones and more polite language.[2]

Children are introduced to these gendered language conventions at a young age through popular culture and their wider environment. By the time they start school, they know how they should speak as a girl or a boy and how to speak to others based on their sex. As they get older, they pick up more language-based gender cues that instill in them an understanding of the expectations placed upon people of their sex. As Allyson Jule, Senior Lecturer in Education at the University of Glamorgan, writes:

> both men and women have been ... instructed and rehearsed (by each other) in the most acceptable ways of talking (just as they have been instructed in the most acceptable ways of dressing) to align with genderedness. ... The acceptance of a 'proper' speech style is ... a symbolic attempt to impose order on the social world. We belong because and when we play by the relevant gender rules.[3]

Along with the behavioural and physical stereotypes discussed in earlier chapters, the language-based stereotypes present in children's popular culture contribute to boys' already distorted ideas about masculinity and femininity.

The Gendered Way We Speak

Biology dictates that women have higher voices than men, but studies have shown that men and women could sound more similar; they just choose not to. Rather, people consciously alter the pitch of their voices to sound more typical of their sex.

This modulation of pitch begins in childhood. In *Girls, Boys and Language,* Joan Swann cites a study in which adults were asked to identify the sex of pre-pubertal children based on their voices alone. The adults answered accurately in most cases. They were able to make a clear distinction between the sexes because boys learn from a young age how to enlarge their vocal tract to produce lower frequencies in their voices, and this difference in tone is readily apparent to others.

Females tend to go the other way. As they mature, many girls and women add elements to their speech that serve to feminize their voices. Some adult women even incorporate into their voices a breathy tone that is unique to the female sex. This breathiness, combined with a higher pitch and tone, make a woman sound girly. Although social conventions teach women to speak in a highly gendered way, this mode of speech does women no favours. In fact, the more feminine a woman sounds, the more negatively she is viewed. Studies have shown that highly feminized voices connote weakness, lack of competence[4] and, in the world of pop culture, frivolousness. (Perhaps these impressions are the reason that 83% of children's films are narrated by males.)[5]

In children's popular culture, highly feminized speaking styles are common in female characters of all ages. Young Isabella in *Phineas and Ferb* speaks in very high, squeaky tones, as does tween Julie from *Bakugan Battle Brawlers*. In the *Mario* series of video games, adult females Daisy and Peach have kewpie doll voices that stand in stark contrast to their male counterparts, Mario and Luigi, whose voices sink into the baritone range. Alex and Clover from *Totally Spies* have very high-pitched, Valley-Girl lilts in their voices. Fiona from the *Shrek* series has a very soft and feminine voice, as does Norma Jean, the mother from *Happy Feet*.

Norma Jean's speech also demonstrates the breathy quality that is common among fictional female characters. Her whispery tones may be intended to underscore the association with iconic namesake Norma Jean Mortenson (Marilyn Monroe), but the end result is an adult woman who sounds like a child.

Like Norma Jean, Daisy, the female cow in *Barnyard* speaks in soft tones with a hint of breathiness, as do Ellie from *Ice Age*, the kung fu masters Tigress and Viper from *Kung Fu Panda*, and Bo Peep from *Toy Story*. The mom in *Grossology*, an otherwise excellent show, speaks in whispery tones with a rather high pitch. The girls in *Spectacular Spider-Man* also speak with soft, breathy voices, except for the intentionally annoying cheerleader, Sally Avril, who uses very shrill tones.

Sally Avril is not the only female character to take her higher pitch to extremes. Many girls do not just have higher voices—they have a grating tone that comes to the fore in the many scenes where they screech and giggle. Candace from *Phineas and Ferb* is one of the best examples. As the older sister she is meant to be the foil for her younger brothers, but her constant shrieking makes her utterly unbearable and a terrible stereotype of teenage girls. Candace is very nearly matched by the *Bakugan* and *Pokemon* girls who shriek and giggle at great volume and with great frequency. Susan and Mary, the older sisters from *Johnny Test*, share Candace's shrill tone at times. Mandy, the nemesis character from *Totally Spies,* speaks in a very screechy voice. Vicky, the nasty babysitter from *The Fairly Odd Parents,* is another female who is prone to shrieking and Mrs. Potato Head from the *Toy Story* series also verges on shrill much of the time.

Pitch is not the only indicator of femininity—the quantity and speed of speech are as well. With their constant chatting and rapid-fire delivery, female characters often reinforce the stereotype of the talkative woman. The comparatively quieter male characters, on the other hand, perpetuate the myth of the strong and silent sex. In the real world, men have been shown to talk more than women,[6] but the stereotype of the chatty female persists in popular culture.

Pepper Potts of *Iron Man: Armored Adventures* is a particularly talkative girl. If she is not constantly chatting at a fast pace, either in-person or via her cell phone, she is texting. Candace talks constantly and is often shown on her cell phone. The three leads from *Totally Spies* speak so fast in some scenes that it is hard to understand what they are saying. In *Toy Story 2*, the increasing age of the girl who owned cowgirl toy Jessie is demonstrated in a scene where she is shown dragging her phone behind her in what appears to be a long phone conversation. While not the worst example of the chatty girl stereotype, it is significant because of the contrast it presents—this kind of image would never be used to signify a boy's progression towards maturity.

Voices indicate strength in the few women who are allowed to appear capable and heroic. Both Wonder Woman and Hawkgirl sound like adult women and speak with confidence. The women of the X-Men also speak with cool competence. Teenaged Gwen Tennyson of *Ben 10: Alien Force* sounds younger than the female Justice Leaguers and X-Men, but she speaks calmly and confidently without ever veering into the screechy tones that characterize other fictional girls her age.

While the tics in female voices are overwhelmingly negative (save for the few hero characters), the speech of male characters also has its share of stereotypes.

Pitch and tone affect males as much as they affect females. Less manly male characters are often given voices with a higher pitch. Both Ziggy from *Power Rangers: RPM* and Marucho from *Bakugan Battle Brawlers* have considerably higher voices than their friends. Marucho is even voiced by a woman.[7] In the various *Scooby-Doo* series, Shaggy's voice has a squeaky tone that marks him as less masculine than Fred, who has a deeper and more even-toned voice. Flint from *Cloudy with a Chance of Meatballs* seems to speak in a fairly standard pitch until he is compared to his father and the town's police chief, both of whom have very deep voices.

And then there are the warrior characters whose voices never break and never betray any sign of weakness. Wolverine speaks with a deep, raspy voice that communicates the barely suppressed rage of his character in *Wolverine and the X-Men*. The moody and intense Batman has a deep voice that is noticeably lower than those of his *Justice League* pals, Superman and The Flash. Bakugan brawlers Dan and Shun, the Power Rangers (minus Ziggy), and Jedi Master Anakin all speak with low voices—relative to their age—that convey authority and self-confidence.

Beyond the sound of male voices, the content of male speech also gives rise to many stereotypes. Studies have shown that, in contrast to females who use more formal or "prestige" language, males are more likely to slip into the vernacular, a casual type of speech that is considered more masculine.[8] In the world of children's popular culture, both male and female characters seem to use relatively informal modes of speaking, but the tendency to go one step beyond the vernacular— into crude or vulgar language—is seen only in male characters.

Puerile or crass language is a hallmark of fictional boys. Some of the worst examples come in the printed word. In the case of the *Captain Underpants* series of books, the title is just the beginning. One book in this series talks about the "Perilous Plot of Professor Poopypants."[9] The character's full name is Pippy P. Poopypants, a name that sends the kids in the book into fits of laughter. Author Dav Pilkey was going for humour here and, as he admits on his website, was not trying to encourage name-calling or any kind of jokes about people's names.[10] While his intentions may be laudable, the names of the book and the series still contribute to the stereotype of the juvenile, potty-mouthed boy.

Another title, published in 2008, hews to the same stereotypes as *Captain Underpants*. Intended for the higher end of the age range I'm discussing here, *Sir Fartsalot Hunts the Booger* features Prince Harry and a flatulent knight who live in the kingdom of Armpit. The story is rife with vulgar language uttered by everyone from the toddler who likes to say "poopy-pantses" to the giant who threatens to clobber a knight to a "glob of guts" and, of course, the mythical "Booger" which is described as making a horrible noise like a "long, liquidy backsnort" and being made "entirely of slimegreen goo."[11]

The language used here is echoed in other series that have truly cringe-inducing passages. Take the various books in the *Time Warp Trio* series. From *Knights of the Kitchen Table*, there is the "long, wet, noisy, and totally disgusting burp" made by a giant or the "green giant slime" that covers people after the giant snorts.[12] From *Tut Tut*, there is the name Hatsnat, which is pronounced "hot snot." The boys in the story amuse themselves by creating variations on this name, including: Cold Boogers, Warm Goober, Hot Slop, and Roasting Goober.[13]

Even the usually polite Geronimo Stilton gets in on the action when he refers to a character as being "puke-green."[14]

That girls rarely, if ever, utter such coarse language is indicative of the stereotypes and resulting double standards that dominate portrayals of gender in popular culture today. Boys, who are considered inherently brattier than girls, are forgiven for talking about poop, snot, and farts while girls, as more delicate creatures, are not allowed to speak of such things.

In addition to crude language, there are other stereotypical signs that a speaker is male. As indicated in a survey of university students cited by Joan Swann, two of the main traits of male speech are aggressive and forceful tones,[15] both of which are evident among the male characters in kids' pop culture.

Aggressive language often takes the form of name-calling. Among mild insults, Timmy from *The Fairly Odd Parents* describes his parents as "dumber than alpacas." Zac Power, lead character in his own book series, refers to his brother as scared, hopeless, and geeky. Buford, the bully character in *Phineas and Ferb* is fond of the word *nerd*.

Stronger insults appear in the *Time Warp Trio* books series, where words like *moron*, *stupid*, and *idiot* are used. (Those terms are largely absent from the TV series based on the books.) The same words are used by the nasty grasshoppers in *A Bug's Life*. In *Bakugan Battle Brawlers*, the word *wuss* is used in reference to a male character[16] and in *Shrek the Third*, Arthur is referred to as a *dork*. In *Sir Fartsalot Hunts the Booger*, the words *loser*, *doofus*, and *buttheaded jerk* are used.

Aggression and force are seen too in certain turns of phrase. Dan from *Bakugan* uses the phrase "You're going down" with great frequency, talks about kicking butt, and, in one episode, tells Julie not to come "crying to him" when he bests her in a Bakugan match.[17] Fred from the *Time Warp Trio* threatens his friends with a "smackdown" while another character tells protagonist Sam to "shut his piehole."[18]

Song lyrics can also take an insulting or aggressive turn. *SpongeBob's Greatest Hits* includes references to idiot friends who slap each other: "Who picks you up and smacks you all around? Idiot friends … Who helps pick your pants up off the ground? Thanks Buddy! Only an idiot would do that."[19]

From the soundtrack of *Phineas and Ferb*, there are references to enemies—"I hate him and he hates me"—and descriptions of bullies as "big and dumb" with brains "the size of a sourdough crumb." For all-out nastiness, there is this lyric from resident evil scientist Dr. Doofenshmirtz: "There are lots of horrid people on this planet that I would love to give a lashing to/But my goody two-shoes brother, the favourite of my mother, is the one I want to smother in a ton of pigeon goo."[20]

While characters like SpongeBob and Doofenshmirtz are using their insults for humour, the fact that the language used here would not be found in cartoons aimed at girls begs the question: why is it okay for boys? This kind of language reinforces the stereotypical image of boys as belligerent and rebellious. It also shows boys that aggressive language is one of the more effective ways for them to differentiate themselves from girls and, in the process, remove any doubt about their masculinity.

Aggressive language is not limited to fictional portrayals. It is heard in the martial language of sports broadcasts—where terms like ammunition, arsenal, attack mode, battle, blast, blitz, detonate, gunning it, reloading, shotgun, sniper, squeeze the trigger, taking aim, and weapons are used[21]—and in advertising for boys' toys, which includes words like deadly, fierce, firepower, force, savage, scorching, and warrior.

These words contrast sharply with the verbiage used in ads for girls' toys. Feminine toys are described with words like beauty, décor, designer, fairy, fashion, girly, glamorous, glittery, gossip, makeovers, pampering, pearlescent, pretty, primping, sassy, shiny, and sparkle.

Even the more mundane toy descriptions hew to stereotypes. The ad copy for the adventure cape I mentioned in chapter 4, while not as aggressive as that for other products, exudes a certain energy: "Shazam! You can have Adventures Galore in this blue Satin cape with a Gold Metallic Orb and twin Silver Metallic Lightening [sic] Bolts!" The description for the Purple Princess Cape has no mention of adventure, noting only that the cape is suitable for "costumes …, dress up parties, weddings and dance recitals."[22]

Producers and marketers may claim that some gender distinctions are needed in their programs and advertising, but by taking language to extremes they perpetuate many of the worst stereotypes of each sex—males are tough and authoritative and women are comparatively weaker, more passive, and more emotional.

Language Used in Reference to Others

The language people use to describe others, whether in a fictional or real-world setting, can contribute to inequality between the sexes as much as the sound of their voices. (Joan Swann would also argue that we can challenge these inequalities through language use, so all is not lost.)[23]

One of the most obvious examples of gender bias in language use is the tendency to discuss females in terms of their appearance and, concurrently, of females to talk about or show concern for how they look. Children are witness to this tendency in popular culture and their everyday lives. On the pop culture side, there are many examples:

- Ellie in *Ice Age 3* talks about the size of her ankles and asks her husband if she looks "round."
- Candace from *Phineas and Ferb* is obsessed with looking good around her crush, Jeremy.
- Kiki in *Kiki's Delivery Service* complains about her ugly dress, comments on the beauty of a female neighbor, and states that she, herself, is "not very beautiful." She also frets about getting fat from eating too many pancakes.
- Daphne of *What's New Scooby-Doo* notes of a female rival that "[a]nyone who wears that much eye shadow is trouble."[24]
- In the various *Pokemon* series, the girls are occasionally complimented on their looks and seem to enjoy the attention, even when it comes from much older men.
- In an episode of *Spectacular Spider-Man*, "nerdette" Gwen Stacy undergoes a kind of makeover, ditching her glasses and pinned back hair. After receiving the predictable

positive reaction from Peter Parker, she decides to keep her new look.

- Like Gwen, Sam from *Cloudy with a Chance of Meatballs* is considered a nerd. She hides her true nature behind a pert TV weather reporter persona. When she reverts to her ponytailed, bespectacled self, Flint tells her that she is now really beautiful. The message about being true to oneself is a good one, but nullified somewhat by the fact that she is judged for her appearance and Flint is not.

As the case of Flint demonstrates, the appearance of male characters is pretty much irrelevant—they do not talk about the way they look and they are rarely described in terms of their appearance. A scan of website profiles of popular characters demonstrates this discrepancy between male and female character descriptions.

The gang from *What's New Scooby-Doo* is one example. Fred is referred to as a leader with "infectious confidence." No mention is made of his appearance. The description of Daphne, on the other hand, notes that she is smart , but only after indicating that she is "beautiful … clothes-conscious and fashionable."[25]

The aforementioned Sam from *Cloudy with a Chance of Meatballs* is first described on the film's website as "cute," while the male characters have no physical description attached to them.[26]

Although they are vehicles, Sally from *Cars* is referred to as beautiful, with her intelligence among the last of her traits mentioned. McQueen, her eventual love interest, is called a hotshot. The other male cars are referred to by their make and model, but not their appearance.[27]

Pepper Potts of *Iron Man: Armored Adventures* is described as "stuck between the tomboy she always was and the pretty young woman she is becoming." No comment is made about the looks of her male friends, Tony and Rhodey.[28]

The tendency to emphasize female appearance exists in people's everyday lives. Adults stress the importance of women's appearance every time they comment on the fashions or overall look of girls and women, be they politicians, celebrities, friends, or family. When children are within earshot, they pick up cues that tell them to place more value on how a woman looks than on what she does. This type of usage is dangerous because it makes a woman a "passive object rather than active subject" while trivializing her and subjecting her to judgments that men do not have to face.[29]

The way people use language also tends to position men as the dominant sex. I used to scoff at so-called politically correct language until I had children and saw the impact of male-centric vocabulary. The use of the words *he, mankind, fireman,* or *policeman* instead of more gender-neutral terms reinforces to boys that being male is the natural state of being.

The tendency for the male to be considered the norm is also evident in the way people use language to mark females. People often feel the need to indicate *female* doctor or *female* police officer, but, because the individuals in those professions are assumed to be male, people feel no need to make such distinctions for their male counterparts. I noticed this tendency to assume maleness in a popular video game. In *MySims:Agents,* children are allowed to create an agent of either sex, but female agents are referred to throughout the game with masculine pronouns and the honorific *Sir.* While surely an oversight by the game's programmers, this mistake reflects the general inclination in children's pop culture to consider males as the default sex.

Words associated exclusively with females can also have a pejorative connotation. The difference in meaning between *master* and *mistress* is one obvious example, but there are many words that, while not defined as feminine, are used solely in reference to girls and women. Words like *shrill*, *gossip*, *catty*, *nag*, *airhead*, and *ditz* are among them, as are the verbs I used earlier—*screech* and *shriek*—which are rarely, if ever, used to describe male speech.

This "semantic pejoration,"[30] as Swann calls it, is apparent in children's popular culture. In multiple episodes of *Bakugan Battle Brawlers*, Dan refers to arguments between girls as "catfights." In a book based on the *Bakguan* series, two female musicians are referred to as "flakes."[31] The princesses in *Sir Fartsalot Hunts the Booger* are described as "tittering like pigeons" and "cooing" at the knights who accompany Prince Harry, and the word "nag" can be heard in reference to female characters in *The Fairly Odd Parents* and *SpongeBob SquarePants*.

The names assigned to female characters can also imply that they lack the strength and importance of male characters. In the *Mario* series of video games, names like Daisy, Peach, Rosalina, and Toadette distinguish the female characters, while the main male characters have names like Mario, Luigi, Wario, and Bowser. While clearly an adult woman, undercover agent Shayera Hol takes the name of Hawkgirl when she finds herself stranded on Earth, a designation that is hard to understand when compared to the names of her male colleagues—alien Kal-el did not choose the name Superboy for his superhero persona, nor did Bruce Wayne settle for Batboy.

The *Geronimo Stilton* series is another case in point. Females—even smart, independent ones—have exceedingly silly names, like Petunia Prettypaws, Pinky Pick, Priscilla Prettywhiskers, Mouselina, and Aunt Sweetfur. On the other hand, women who are intended as villains or nuisance characters have less pretty names—like Tina Spicytail and Sally Ratmousen.

Male characters in this series occasionally have funny monikers, but their names have far different connotations than the female names. Typical male names include Hercule Poirat, Bruce Hyena, Uncle Grayfur, Kornelius von Kickpaw, and Henry Handipaws, a custodian who works with the teacher Miss Angel Paws. For the record, recent titles in this series show no sign of improvement. *The Kingdom of Fantasy*, released in 2009, includes a character called Princess Scatterbrain who is described as "a bit on the ditzy side," in contrast to King Factual, who likes science and loves to read.[32]

Overall, the language used to describe males and females in children's popular culture continues the same trends seen elsewhere—diminishing the feminine while positioning males as the stronger and more important sex.

Gender Bias in What Children See and Hear

When considering the impact of language on perceptions of gender, I recall the words of journalism professor Justin Lewis, first cited in the introduction to this book: "The way media influences the way we think … is much more a question of creating a certain environment of images that we grow up in and that we become used to and after a while those images will begin to shape what we know and what we understand about the world."[33]

That environment is not just a visual one—it is also an auditory one. In this environment, every feminized voice (whether in a male or female character), every aggressive word uttered by a gravelly-voiced alpha male, every comment about the way a girl or woman looks, and every gender-specific insult reinforces the gender stereotypes already made evident through the appearance and behaviour of fictional characters.

Writer Rita Mae Browne once wrote that language "exerts hidden power, like the moon on the tides."[34]

Indeed, language has so subtle an impact that its influence on a boy's ideas about gender may go unnoticed. Because it underlies everything I discussed in the previous chapters—the dialogue and descriptions of fictional characters, the text that embellishes children's clothing, and the copy used in toy advertising—it is imperative that we pay attention to the messages it conveys.

Chapter 7: What We Can Do About the Achilles Effect

Is the Achilles Effect real? Is it possible for young boys to grasp all of the negative messages about gender in the popular culture and wider environment that surround them? So little research has been done on boys and gender perceptions that it is hard to tell, but here are a couple of statements about gender from a random sampling of nine-year-old girls:

- "There are different jobs for boys—like doctors are usually for boys and that's why they make nurses, for girls. There's always different stuff for boys and girls."
- "Girls do the housecleaning and taking care of babies. If the woman goes out, babies don't get care and dads don't know how to cook and they'll be starving."[1]

Although these comments sound like they were made decades ago, they were actually reported in the *Toronto Star* in January of 2010. That's right. Girls in 2010 still believe that doctors are more likely to be male and that fathers are not capable of fulfilling the basic needs of their children. And if girls think that way, it is reasonable to assume that boys, who are exposed to many of the same influences, share their feelings.

Still more examples abound in conversations overheard among parents, paraphrased here:

- "I think it's different for boys. They have trouble sitting still in school."
- "I'm sure this doesn't happen in the boys' locker room, but the girls were all sobbing and crying after they lost the game."
- "Isn't it nice to know your son isn't the only one who doesn't listen? They're all like that."

From a blog called *Radical Parenting*, a 17-year-old girl wrote this passage before encouraging parents to cease and desist with traditional gender roles:

- "Little girls are expected to act a certain way and little boys another ... Children are quick to learn their roles. Part of the growing process is to emulate what they see. Little girls familiarize with their mothers and begin to act like mommy. Boys as we know are taught the complete opposite. They can be messy and rude with very little repercussions. They can get away with anything. They do as dear old dad does."[2]

Given this evidence, the short answer to the question that opens this chapter is, yes, the Achilles Effect is real.

Boys continue to be surrounded by images of the ideal man as physically strong, emotionally detached, and disinclined toward parenting or anything else that requires him to show vulnerability or deep affection. Even if young boys cannot comprehend the wider meaning of what they see, they will have a mental storehouse of clues and cues to apply to the situations they face as they get older.

In the preface I mentioned the stark contrast between preschool and school-age TV programs. As boys enter the middle school years, they will encounter yet another abrupt shift in the tone of the pop culture that surrounds them. Their ideas about masculinity and femininity will be challenged by popular sitcoms that trade on the idea of the dopey dad who cannot function without Mom. Music will start to exert some influence, as will music videos. (Depending on the artist, the lyrics and content of music videos can be extremely misogynistic.) Movies, which already set a poor example for young kids, will continue to show boys a world dominated by men.

As parents, we need to make sure our sons are properly equipped to deal with the images they see as they move through childhood. As with all types of learning, a good foundation is the key and that is what *The Achilles Effect* is about—establishing a balanced perspective on gender that boys can carry with them into adolescence and adulthood.

There are parallels here to other childhood lessons. We teach our children manners. We teach them to share. We teach them that bullying is wrong. Similarly, we should teach them about the hazards of gender stereotypes. Our sons need to know that media characterizations of men and women are, at best, exaggerated and, at worst, blatantly sexist. They need to understand that the image of boys created by marketers is not representative of boys in general. And they need the confidence to be themselves and follow their own interests, whether that means playing hockey or playing house.

Establishing gender balance requires us to be aware of our own biases, which are sometimes difficult to recognize. Even the most gender-conscious parents may unwittingly send signals that reinforce gender roles. In her book *Delusions of Gender*, psychologist Cordelia Fine notes that parents' behaviour toward their babies is influenced by their own gender stereotypes, even if those stereotypes are only implicitly held. The words and non-verbal cues of parents send strong messages about what types of behaviour are acceptable, and these messages are readily understood by babies and toddlers. For example: parents may unknowingly speak in unenthusiastic tones or withdraw attention when a child does something that does not align with their idea of appropriate gender behaviour; they tend to surround children with toys that suit their gender; and they often dress their children according to gender norms about colour and imagery (no trucks for girls, no rainbows and unicorns for boys).

In short, parents tag gender and "draw attention to gender as an important way of dividing the social world into categories." In so doing, they set their young children up to "seize on any element that may implicate a gender norm so that they may categorize it as male or female."[3]

I have had such experiences with my own children. One day I needed to reach something on a high shelf in our garage. Having never seen me climb a ladder before, my younger son asked me as I took my first step whether "womans can climb ladders." He has also asked me if women drink coffee, since I do not but my husband does. I shudder to think about his opinion of female drivers—he has seen me crash into the recycling bins a number of times, but Daddy never has. (These incidents came about not because I am a female driver, but because, after many years using public transit as my main mode of conveyance, I am not a very experienced driver.)

None of these actions—climbing ladders, drinking coffee, or smacking the blue box with the car—have anything to do with gender, but my son is so keen to understand what *man* and *woman* mean that he will assign gender to even the most mundane activities. His inclination to define activities as *male* or *female*, and his brother's before him, came about despite my husband's and my awareness of gender bias and attempts to avoid it. (As Fine notes in her book, the gender dividing line appears even when it is not consciously drawn by parents.)

Now imagine what happens when a boy's natural curiosity about gender and his instinct to associate repeated behaviours with a certain sex are combined with the messages delivered by popular culture. If he can assume from seeing his father drink coffee everyday that coffee consumption is a masculine activity, what is he learning from TV, books, films, and toys, which promote gender stereotypes at every turn? Here are the lessons, summarized from the preceding chapters and written in something approximating a young boy's language:

Boys are strong, girls are less so. Smart guys aren't as cool as tough guys. Girls cry and giggle and screech a lot. Tough boys get angry easily but that just shows how strong they are. Dads get angry with their sons a lot and sometimes just leave. Girls are good at being moms and taking care of dads and kids. There are more stories about boys because they are more interesting than girls, maybe because girls don't do fun stuff—they just dress up and play with Barbies. Girls can't rescue people. Heroes have big muscles and beat up the bad guys. Boys can be bratty and use yucky language, but girls can't talk like that. Girls can play with dolls, wear pink, dress up as princesses, and play house, but boys should never do those things because they'll look girly.

All of these pieces of the gender puzzle merge in a boy's mind as he tries to deduce what *boy* and *girl* mean. As I mentioned in the introduction, the final picture is not a pretty one.

To change the gender picture that many boys draw for themselves, we need to: create an environment in which women and men are shown as equally competent, capable, and intelligent; minimize stereotypical portrayals of men and highlight positive male role models; and, most importantly, get involved and engaged in what our sons are reading and watching so we can help them negotiate a fictional world where images of males and females continue to be badly distorted.

In so doing, we can help alter the definition of masculinity, a term whose current meaning imposes far too many limitations on boys. With masculinity redefined, boys will be: less troubled by expressing emotion; less inclined to false bravado and macho posturing; and more confident in their choices about books, toys, films, and, eventually, careers because they will not feel hemmed in by gender.

Boys raised under this new definition of masculinity will feel less self-conscious about taking on "women's" activities as they get older. They will also value the role, work, and opinions of women and girls and see sexual equality as a desirable goal. And they will look at Achilles and his ilk as a relic of another time, when physical strength, aggression, and desire for dominance were the sole signifiers of manhood and masculinity.

Taking Action

There are many ways that we, as parents, can teach our sons greater gender sensitivity and introduce more gender balance to their lives. In this section, I have outlined some concrete steps you can take in this direction. I will occasionally refer to specific TV programs, movies, and books as examples. A complete list of titles is available in the Recommended Resources chapter.

Start Young

It is never too early to set a good example for your son. When he is in the preschool age range, include a variety of characters in his TV viewing and reading. Focus on male and female protagonists or programs and books with a group of male and female friends, like *Arthur* or *Franklin the Turtle*. Fortunately, with preschool books and television, gender balance is fairly easy to find.

Watch, Then Share

When children start school they encounter the marketing juggernaut that has brought the faces of SpongeBob, Batman, Spider-Man, and Ben 10 to everything from backpacks and lunch bags to T-shirts and socks. They will be introduced to characters they have never seen before through toys that other kids bring to school. While it is easy to just go along and buy the toys or rent the videos, you may end up inadvertently exposing your son to images that you would rather he not see.

Before letting him watch a new video or TV show, take the time to watch an episode or two yourself. Be sure to watch not just the main characters, but the supporting characters and images. Listen to the language. Is there sexist or demeaning language used in reference to a character, like the "nagging" wife on *SpongeBob SquarePants* or the "catfighting" girls on *Bakugan*? Are there familiar stereotypes? The buff and burly hero or the small and skinny nerd? Look at some of the other themes I discussed here. How are parents portrayed? Are females, if they are present, restricted to secondary roles? Is violence used to solve problems?

Being familiar with the content will help you decide whether the program is appropriate. It will also give you a chance to understand the basic story so you can find alternatives that might be equally appealing to your son. For example, if he likes action, you can direct him toward a show like *Grossology* where there is little violence, but lots of excitement.

Remember that vigilance is a parent's best friend. Many adults are unaware of the gender bias in kids' popular culture, especially as it affects males. Watching the programs your son likes can really open your eyes to the messaging in kids' films and TV shows.

Talk to Your Son

Being aware of what your child is watching is only the first step. You must also talk to him about the content.

Ask him a few questions before he watches a new show. What does he know about the program? What is it about the show that appeals to him? Is it the main character? Is it a supporting character? Is it the adventures the characters go on? By learning what he wants in a program, you may be able to turn his attention toward an alternative that you find more suitable and that will still entertain him.

If you are not comfortable with the language or images in the program, you have a choice between banning it outright and allowing limited access to the show. If you have decided the show is off-limits, explain that it is not appropriate for him and offer him an alternative, if possible.

If you decide to allow some access, watch with him to gauge his reaction and to discuss the program afterwards. Not only will you begin to teach him about gender balance, you will also provide him with some valuable lessons in media awareness, including the fact that just because something is on TV does not mean it is acceptable or right.

There is no need to be heavy-handed with the questioning and discussion. Even brief chats will open your son's mind to the fact that the fictional worlds he sees portrayed on television are very different from the real world. It is important to let him know that there is nothing wrong with an escapist story, but that the norms and behaviours that apply in those worlds do not necessarily apply in ours. Here are a few key discussion points you can use, adapting the conversation to his level.

- How does he feel about the male lead? Do other boys at school talk like that character or act like that character? This question will help him realize that boys are not nearly as one-dimensional as their media portrayals would indicate.
- Relate the male lead to him. If he were in the same situation, would he act like the male lead? What would

he do differently? With this question, your son will realize that there are different ways to solve problems and that the characters on TV may not always make the best choices.

- If there are few or no girls, ask him about that too. Where are the girls? Why are there no girls on that show, but lots in his class at school? Using this kind of questioning, you will introduce him to the idea that TV is not like the real world, which includes males and females in equal numbers.

- With an older child, you can begin discussions about how boys and girls are portrayed. In an action/adventure show, ask him why he thinks the boys like to fight so much. If the male characters are stereotypically tough, ask your son if he thinks they get scared or tired or maybe just want a break from all that hero stuff. By humanizing the characters in this way, you can make them seem more realistic, while letting your son know that it is okay to be afraid or upset or to simply want time away from life's demands.

- Highlight the good aspects of the show so your son begins to recognize positive gender role models. Nemo's father clearly loves his son. Shun in *Bakugan* takes care of his mother when she is ill. Brock in *Pokemon* watches over his younger siblings. Abby and Ty of *Grossology* work together to solve crimes. Examples like these show boys in a different light and are important for young boys to see.

- Wherever there are positive lessons—even in programs you do not favour—be sure to point them out. Tell your son that while you do not agree with the fighting and violence superheroes use, you understand that they are honourable people who have made it their mission to help others. Talk about how Anakin is a good teacher to Ahsoka or how Ben Tennyson respects his cousin Gwen and girlfriend Julie. Emphasizing the positive not only outweighs the negative messages in the program, it also shows that you are making an effort to support your son's interests instead of demonizing the characters and programs he likes.

The strategies I outlined above apply equally to books which, unlike television, are essential to your son's development. Read with your child and discuss the content to ensure the good messages in a book are not obscured by the bad. And remember, with issues of gender, it is all about balance.

As an example, I can point to my own experience with the *Geronimo Stilton* series. I panned that series earlier but I should disclose that my son has read practically all of the books. Knowing that no book or TV show is perfect, I have allowed this less-than-ideal series because he enjoys it so much. I have discussed my concerns with him and have made sure to compensate for its stereotyped characters with other materials that offer better gender portrayals.

A Strategy for Superheroes

As I mentioned in earlier chapters, superheroes have a way of infiltrating the minds of little boys. The new breed of action heroes, who are not necessarily "super"—like Ben Tennyson of *Ben 10:Alien Force* and Anakin Skywalker of *Star Wars: The Clone Wars*—have a similar effect.

For many parents, these characters present a challenge: how do you permit your son some degree of access to the characters without exposing him to the violence that dominates the television shows and movies about them?

If you find yourself in this situation, you could go the "small dose" route and allow your son to see an occasional episode as a treat, watching with him to mediate the violence and other negative messages.

You could also direct your son's attention to books, where the violence is less visceral. Superhero books are not without their flaws—

women are highly sexualized and male figures are badly distorted—so you may want to read them before giving them to your son. There are superhero books for virtually all reading levels, including early reader books based on Spider-Man and Batman, so you may find some that are acceptable for your son.

You may also be able to appease your son with toys that enable him to pretend he is his favourite character. Even action figures, as physically distorted as they are, may be a better solution than the far too realistic animated programs.

The lack of women in superhero stories is getting easier to combat thanks to the inclusion of more female heroes in new *Justice League* and *X-Men* series. Still, it may help to highlight the powers of the women. In stories where women do not play a part, you can point out their absence and then engage your son in a conversation about how a female hero would have handled the problem. Kids love talking to their parents about these kinds of things, if for no other reason than to demonstrate their knowledge of the fictional worlds they've seen portrayed.

Take a situation, say when Green Lantern traps a bad guy, and point out how Wonder Woman would have saved the day or what Storm or Jean Grey from the X-Men would have done. Of course, you will have to do some research into these female characters, but even cursory knowledge will suffice. Your son will love learning about the superpowers that other characters possess, regardless of their gender, and you will share in a great conversation that gives your son a chance to exercise his imagination.

Body Image

As the chapter on superheroes and sports stars showed, unrealistic body proportions in male characters can be just as damaging as those in female characters.

Although the impact may not be felt until the middle school years or adolescence, it is during early childhood that boys begin to understand the supposed importance of being muscular and physically strong. That being said, it is never too early to help your son develop a positive body image.

- Model good behaviour. Try not to make statements about the appearance of others.
- Comments about how little, thin, or heavy a boy is may be interpreted by him as a negative, so focus more on his abilities and not his size.
- Check your own language when watching sports with your son and try not to be overly critical of players who perform badly. It sounds clichéd, but try to emphasize that making the effort is more important than winning.
- Try to show your son athletes who excel without being built like action figures. Because they require agility, baseball infield players are often less bulked up, as are tennis players and figure skaters.
- Highlight good sportsmanship and explain that playing fair is of more value than simply winning.
- Showcase athletes who do good deeds in their community to demonstrate that athletes have interests other than sports.
- Read stories about men doing more than using their brute strength. There are biographies of all kinds of accomplished men available in a wide range of reading levels. Einstein, Da Vinci (even featured in a *Magic Tree House* story), and various male astronauts are among those that may intrigue young boys.
- Studies have shown that boys like seeing characters solve problems. Choose stories that involve problem solving without a physical resolution. In so doing, you will highlight thinking, compassion, and other non-physical strengths.

The *Brady Brady* series of books is good for younger readers and *The Magic Tree House* series is great for older readers.

Teach Advertising Savvy

Television and websites come with advertising, and lots of it. While too much talk can overwhelm your child, you may want to add some references to advertising in your discussions with him. He needs to know the real purpose of advertising—manufacturing an ideal play environment, complete with the latest toys, in order to get parents to spend money.

In creating this ideal, advertisers appeal to the basest and most stereotypical aspects of maleness. What boy wouldn't want a Nerf machine gun that fires darts at a rate of three per second[4] or a G.I. Joe action figure with crossbow, nunchuks, or explosive devices? By hewing to conventional views of masculinity, advertisers make these toys seem like an essential part of boyhood. Teaching your son about the gender bias inherent in toy advertising will help him see these marketing pitches for what they really are and provide him with a healthy dose of scepticism about advertising in general.

- Explain that advertisements for boys' toys pigeonhole boys into certain types of behaviour, often violent and aggressive. As with the discussion on television above, make him aware that boys are not all the same and that he does not have to like a toy just because it is popular or because it seems to be a "must-have" for boys. A scary toy like Bionicles may be offputting for a youngster, and he needs to know that it is okay to prefer a different kind of toy.
- Point out the differences between commercials for boys' toys and those for girls' toys. The former tends to be noisy with lots of primary colours, while the latter tends to be quieter and doused in purple and pink. Ask him why he

thinks boys' toys are always about loud battles. Ask him if he thinks a girl would be interested in Hot Wheels or Bakugan toys, and, if so, why commercials make those toys seem appropriate only for boys. You can also try the reverse—ask him why baby dolls are shown as being only for girls when young boys like to play with them. Again, you will reinforce to him that the things he sees on television are not an accurate reflection of the real world.

- If he comments that a toy looks fun, ask him what is fun about it. By understanding which aspects of a toy appeal to him, you can direct him elsewhere or point out that he already has a toy with those characteristics. You can also launch a talk about the nature of the toy (violent, juvenile, puerile) and why you would prefer him not to play with it.

- Above all, be an engaged consumer. If you do not like the messaging in a toy ad, don't buy the product. If you want to take further action, write a letter or blog about what you see. If enough people speak out, toy makers and marketers will start paying attention and, hopefully, change their ways.

Create Balance

One of the best ways to combat gender bias is to introduce more balanced gender portrayals into your son's life. As I noted earlier, it is best to start at a young age. Including women in your son's world view helps combat the pop culture trend of male dominance. If he is hesitant—believing that a toy, book, or film is for girls—you may need to resort to bribery.

- Start by pointing out the females that are present in a book or program—even if their role is small—and make them part of the story. Ask questions about female characters or talk about what they are doing to draw attention to them.

- If he is reluctant to read a book or watch a program with a female in a major role, dare him. Make it a game. Ask him to read the book or watch the show with a promise to make his favourite dessert if he really doesn't like it. Start with something he is bound to enjoy, like the *Magic Tree House* books or *Grossology*. From there you can move on to a female-centred book or program.

- After you have read a few books or watched a few shows that feature females in major roles, have a discussion about how similar the characters are to him. Elizabeth in *The Paper Bag Princess* is courageous and clever; Annie in the *Magic Tree House* series is fun and adventurous; Olivia has endless energy; Judy Moody likes to collect dead moths and band-aids and has aspirations to be a doctor; Betty on *Atomic Betty* is smart and can outwit the bad guys. Discussions like this make it clear that girls and boys are not as different as your son might have been led to believe.

- Point out characters or situations that deviate from the norm. Robert Munsch books include some great examples: a boy who likes to wear pink, a dad cooking dinner, and a female hockey player who builds her own rink on a river. The idea is to accentuate the varying roles that men, women, boys, and girls play in their everyday lives.

- For boys who are sports fans, try to introduce female athletes into the mix. Olympic events offer great opportunities to do this, but even outside of those competitions you can discuss women's basketball, hockey, figure skating, curling, and tennis. Point out stories in the paper or read non-fiction books about women who have excelled in sports, like hockey player Hayley Wickenheiser, race car driver Danica Patrick, or tennis stars Venus and Serena Williams.

Emphasize Non-Traditional Behaviour

It is important for boys to grow up with the idea there is no such thing as gendered behaviour. Just as girls are capable of being scientists, engineers, or truck drivers, boys can be nurses, teachers, and stay-at-home dads, and contribute to the household by cooking, cleaning, and doing other tasks often associated with females.

- For a younger boy, take all available opportunities to enhance imaginative play and move him in new directions. Play "chef" and teach him to bake cookies. Use a tea set or pots and pans to prepare and serve a meal. Allow female figures (Playmobil, Fisher-Price, Lego) to do non-traditional things, like drive a fire truck or fly a plane.
- Involve an older boy in household tasks like folding laundry, helping with the dishes, or setting the table so he understands that these things are done by everyone, not just mothers.
- Encourage boys of all ages to sit down to quiet activities that do not involve hyperkinetic video games or TV shows. Crafts and building toys are great for a boy's attention span and his motor skills. The act of creating something, whether a painting or a Lego structure, will also do wonders for his self-esteem and confidence.
- Read non-fiction stories about women so boys can understand that people of both sexes can achieve great things. I mentioned female sports stars earlier. You could also include books about women like Amelia Earheart, astronauts Roberta Bondar and Sally Ride, or Jane Goodall.
- Try to include positive portrayals of fathers in your selections as well. In the Recommended Resources in the next chapter I have listed some, but more are starting to appear as the issues surrounding negative portrayals of fathers gain traction in our popular culture.

Non-traditional behaviour extends to the emotional realm. Begin the process of open communication at a young age, including your talks about media and books. Encourage a boy to discuss things that are bothering him, no matter how trivial they might seem. If he begins to talk about something that is weighing on him, stop what you are doing and listen. Do not judge—let him say what is on his mind. He needs to feel safe and comfortable so he can understand that talking about problems is the best way to handle them. And be generous with physical affection. Offer lots of hugs and cuddles to make him feel secure and to help him realize that being obvious about your affection for others is not girly.

Last Words

Those who believe in nature over nurture will tell us that boys are inherently competitive and aggressive, loud, and belligerent. The science on that is dubious and the anecdotal evidence is even more so.

Look around any schoolyard or playground and you will see tremendous diversity in attitude and behaviour among the boys. Some will sit quietly digging in the dirt, imagining that they are uncovering an ancient civilization. Some will improvise a game of *Star Wars* on the climber, focusing on strategy and battle plans. Some will play a game of hockey or soccer. Some will avoid female contact and some will engage in play with the girls in their class or play group.

With such a range of behaviour, how can anyone say that gender is an accurate predictor of a boy's actions and reactions?

Yet that is exactly the message we get from our popular culture and wider society. The male of our species is restricted to certain types of "manly" behaviour and barred from any actions that may be deemed too feminine.

By reading this book and taking action—even if you make just a few small changes—you will help alter the perceptions that many boys have of men as tough guys devoid of emotion, utterly incompetent parents, or rule-breaking slackers. You will also teach them to value the many contributions that women make to our world.

In the process, you will blur, if not erase altogether, the line that so sharply divides masculinity and femininity—a line that emphasizes the differences between the sexes instead of the commonalities, elevates one sex and diminishes the other, and creates artificial boundaries that restrict the possibilities and potential of both boys and girls.

Chapter 8: Recommended Resources

This chapter has two parts. The first section, for parents, includes online and print resources that discuss gender stereotyping and media awareness. The second part, for children and parents, introduces children's programs, films, and books with good gender portrayals.

This list of recommended books, films, and television shows is far from comprehensive and very subjective. It is meant to serve only as a starting point for parents who want to add some gender balance to their sons' entertainment. The materials I have selected here demonstrate what a balanced, or nearly balanced, program or book looks like. Lists are sorted alphabetically by author, organization, or, in the case of animated programs, by title.

As I discover new items I will add them to my blog at www.achilleseffect. com.

For Parents

Websites

The Achilles Effect, www.achilleseffect.com.
My own blog where I review films, books, and television shows and share news related to boys, masculinity, and gender.

Adios Barbie, www.adiosbarbie.com

Adios Barbie promotes healthy body image for girls, boys, men, and women. The site shares news, opinion, and a good number of resources about body image and body esteem.

Canadian Association for the Advancement of Women and Sport and Physical Activity, www.caaws.ca/e/index.cfm.

CAAWS is an organization that seeks an equitable sport and physical activity system in which girls are actively engaged as leaders and participants. The Resources and Publications section on their site includes a report on sex discrimination in sports.

Center for Media Literacy, www.medialit.org.

This wide-ranging site promotes media literacy education. Under Media Issues/Topics, visitors can select from many subject areas, including stereotyping.

Children Now, http://www.childrennow.org/index.php/learn/reports and research/article/226.

This link highlights a research report done by Children Now on media messages about masculinity. The organization has done plenty of research in other areas, including health and education.

Common Sense Media, www.commonsensemedia.org.

Although it is not solely about gender, this website provides reviews and commentary about children's films, television shows, books, and music. The site's operators offer their own opinions and allow parents and kids to contribute too. It is easy to navigate and is always current. I use this site on a regular basis.

Geena Davis Institute on Gender in Media,
http://www.thegeenadavisinstitute.org/research.php.

> Although focused on girls, this site offers research into gender imbalance in popular children's films.

The Hathor Legacy, http://thehathorlegacy.com/.

> The Hathor Legacy "searches for good female characters" in all media. Its home page is easily navigated, with categories for movies, television, books, and other entertainment. Each category is then broken down into various genres. Reviews offer descriptions of how females are portrayed. The many comments for each post offer further insight and perspective.

International Central Institute for Youth and Educational Television,
http://www.br-online.de/jugend/izi/english/home.htm.

> This organization with a rather long name (thankfully shortened to IZI) is a treasure trove of studies on children and television. IZI has done a lot of research into what children watch and how they interpret the messages they see. The site can be a little cumbersome to navigate. Its research section is the best place to start. For research into gender, use this link: http://www.br-online.de/jugend/izi/english/research/research.htm#gender.

Marketing, Media and Childhood,
http://www.marketingmediachildhood.com/

> This blog features commentary and news about harmful messages communicated to children through the media in all of its forms.

Media Awareness Network, www.media-awareness.ca.

> This Canadian site includes a collection of resources for parents and teachers designed to help teach children media awareness. Subjects covered include stereotyping, violence, online hate, and information privacy. This site contains a lot of research, a blog, and a resource catalogue.

Media Education Foundation, http://www.mediaed.org/.

The Media Education Foundation produces top-notch documentaries about media issues, including the widely watched *Killing Us Softly: Advertising's Image of Women* and *Mickey Mouse Monopoly: Disney, Childhood & Corporate Power*. DVDs are priced for educational institutions but full transcripts can be downloaded for free. The site also contains study guides and handouts for teachers.

National Institute on Media + The Family, http://www.mediafamily.org/about/index.shtml.

This site is home to an American group dedicated to researching and raising awareness of the impact of media on children. "Hot topics" on this site include body image, violence, addiction, and brain development.

Pigtail Pals, http://blog.pigtailpals.com/

Pigtail Pals, the business, manufactures empowering clothing for girls. *Pigtail Pals*, the blog, offers trenchant commentary on gender discrimination in popular culture and advertising.

Shaping Youth, www.shapingyouth.org.

Always thought provoking, this site is a forum about the influence of media and marketing on today's children.

Women's Sports Foundation, www.womenssportsfoundation.org.

An American organization founded by tennis legend Billie Jean King, the Women's Sports Foundation advocates for equality and promotes sports and physical activity for girls and women. Their position statement on media images and the words used to describe female athletes shows how far women's sports have to go to achieve parity with men's.

Books

Durham, M. Gigi. *The Lolita Effect: The Media Sexualization of Young Girls and What We Can Do About It*. Woodstock: Overlook Press, 2008.

> *The Lolita Effect* inspired more than the title of my book. In examining media portrayals of females, it motivated me to write a book on a similar subject for young boys. Durham's book talks about sexualized images of females in advertising and pop culture. I highly recommend it for parents of girls as a tool for teaching their daughters about stereotyped and sexualized portrayals of women and girls in the media. I also recommend it for parents of boys as a thorough introduction to media literacy and awareness, which is something children of both sexes need.

Fine, Cordelia. *Delusions of Gender*. New York: W.W. Norton & Company, 2010.

> This book had just been published as I finished writing my own. I concede that I have not read it in its entirety—I was afraid of overlap between it and what I had written in *The Achilles Effect*. But the introduction and couple of chapters I did read point to an entertaining book that completely debunks the myth that men's and women's brains are wired differently, instead naming culture as the primary agent in creating gender differences.

Kindlon, Dan and Michael Thompson. *Raising Cain: Protecting the Emotional Life of Boys*. New York: Random House, 2000.

> This book cautions parents not to fall into the trap of stunting their sons' emotional growth by toughening them with harsh discipline and lack of affection. It also advises parents not to accept an outmoded definition of manhood that focuses on physical strength, aggression, stoicism, and emotional distance.

Madrid, Mike. *The Supergirls: Fashion, feminism, fantasy and the history of comic book heroines*. Minneapolis: Exterminating Angel Press, 2009.

> For anyone interested in superheroes, this book is a lot of fun to read. It is also a great backgrounder for parents who want to introduce female superheroes to their sons.

Pope, Harrison et al. *The Adonis Complex*. New York: Touchstone, 2000.

> This book offers a detailed look at body image issues among boys and men, with a focus on how body dissatisfaction has increased among males since the 1980s. There is a chapter dedicated to boys that talks about the extent of body image problems and the use of steroids and supplements. Chapter 2 includes images that demonstrate just how much the male ideal has changed since the use of anabolic steroids took hold among body builders, athletes, actors, and models.

Silverstein, Olga and Beth Rashbaum. *The Courage to Raise Good Men*. New York: Penguin Books, 1994.

> An excellent book that talks about the push to make little boys into men at a young age, *The Courage to Raise Good Men* challenges the belief that mothers need to pull back from their sons in order to ensure they become "real" men—a belief that is still common today, despite greater general awareness of the emotional needs of boys.

For Children

I have divided this section by media. Although *The Achilles Effect* talks about early school-age boys, I have included a few titles that will appeal to preschoolers and kindergartners alike.

Picture Books

While it is difficult to find consistently excellent gender portrayals in each and every work, I have highlighted books whose strong lead characters and good stories negate any stereotyping they might have. Some of the chapter books may be challenging for a boy to read, but are great for parents to read to their sons.

Cottringer, Anne. *Eliot Jones, Midnight Superhero*. Toronto. Scholastic Canada Ltd., 2008.

> The protagonist in this book is quite unlike other superheroes. For starters, he is small and proudly wears glasses. There is no ditching the specs à la Clark Kent here. While some of his feats involve physical prowess—skiing down glaciers and swimming through "towering waves"—in his most dramatic rescue, it is his brain and not his brawn that saves the day. The insides of the front and back covers display graph paper with Eliot's big invention sketched out—evidence of a creative and clever boy. Yes, there are elements of the stereotypical fearless boy in this story, but the moral of the story is that thinking can solve just as many problems as physical force. And that is a message that all boys can stand to hear.

Donaldson, Julia. *The Snail and the Whale*. London: Macmillan Children's Books, 2003.

> Donaldson is perhaps best known for her book *The Gruffalo*, a great story for young kids. I love *The Snail and the Whale* for the illustrations, its environmental message, and for the fact that the tiny snail with a huge sense of adventure is identified as "she." The female teacher in this book is a bit of a stereotype, but the overall story of a snail seeking an exciting adventure trumps the strict, matronly teacher who turns pale at the sight of the snail. This book, written in rhyme, will appeal to children of both sexes.

Gay, Marie-Louise. *When Stella Was Very, Very Small*. Toronto: Groundwood Books, 2009.

> This title is the latest in a series of books based on the character of Stella. Ideal for the pre-kindergarten to kindergarten age, this series

offers an imaginative and thoughtful female protagonist who interacts lovingly with her inquisitive younger brother. The illustrations are wonderful and the text is intelligent and fun. This author has written equally good books about Stella's younger brother, Sam.

Gillmor, Don. *Sophie and the Sea Monster*. Toronto: Scholastic Canada Inc., 2005.

This is another book with a female protagonist whose story will appeal to children of both sexes. Sophie finds a sea monster under her bed and, after overcoming her fears, she confronts him, befriends him, and helps him conquer his fear of water so he can return home to the sea. Sophie's older brother is a bit bratty, but he is countered by a positive image of a father. (Note that some youngsters may be frightened by the full-page image of an open-mouthed shark.)

Hutchins, Hazel and Gail Herbert. *Mattland*. Toronto: Annick Press, 2008.

With research showing that boys tend to like stories where the main character overcomes a challenge, this book is ideal. The protagonist is a young boy who has moved from town to town and finds himself in a new neighbourhood that he dislikes. It is abundantly clear that Matt is frustrated and angry, but he vents these emotions in a positive way. He uses found objects to create his own playland. When an outsider, who happens to be female, enters his land, he somewhat reluctantly accepts her offer of a Popsicle stick. When she returns, he welcomes her participation in building Mattland. In the end, other children from the neighbourhood join in to save Mattland from a sudden downpour.

Mattland scores high points for showing a boy using his imagination and creativity as an outlet for his emotions. The gender of the "outsider" is never an issue. Matt clearly has no problem playing with girls, and the book demonstrates that girls can build cities just as well as boys.

Johnson, Crockett. *Harold and the Purple Crayon*. New York: HarperCollins, 1955.

> The protagonist in this book is a gentle and imaginative boy who creates entirely new worlds with his purple crayon. The story is inspiring to children and Harold is an excellent role model for boys.

Mazer, Anne. *The Salamander Room*. New York: Dragonfly Books, 1991.

> Another tale of a boy with a vivid imagination, *The Salamander Room* tells the story of a boy who brings home a salamander and dreams of transforming his room into a suitable environment for his new friend. The protagonist is very thoughtful and caring, and, like Harold, another excellent role model for boys.

Munsch, Robert and Askar, Saoussan. *Munschworks 4*. Toronto: Annick Press Ltd., 2002.

> The title above refers to a collection of Robert Munsch books, but all of the Munsch books I have read score high marks for including equal numbers of male and female characters and for showing fathers in a positive light. Favourites in our house include *Just One Goal*, *Fifty Below Zero*, *Pigs*, and *Andrew's Loose Tooth*, which includes perhaps the hippest rendition of the tooth fairy in children's literature.
>
> (There is one possible exception in the Munsch oeuvre. As mentioned earlier, *Love You Forever*, although popular, has been interpreted by some as showing an extremely overprotective mother.)

Rey, Margaret and H.A. *A Treasury of Curious George*. New York: Houghton Mifflin, 2004.

> *Curious George* has been around for some seventy years. The reasons for his longevity are obvious: the stories are fun to read and have subtle lessons about what can happen when someone is too curious.

The little monkey and his caretaker, The Man with the Yellow Hat, are both good role models—caring, gentle and, in the case of the man, extremely patient.

Newer titles, written in the style of Margaret and H.A. Rey, continue the tradition of the series. One of our current favourites is *Curious George Plants a Tree*.

Reynolds, Peter H. *The Dot*. Cambridge, MA: Candlewick Press, 2003.
This is a simple story about encouraging artistic exploration in children. The female protagonist, Vashti, believes she cannot draw. When her teacher tells her to "make a mark and see where it takes [her]" she makes a single dot out of sheer frustration, but then discovers that she can paint.

Reynolds also wrote *Ish*, a story in which a boy named Ramon, initially discouraged by his brother's ridicule of his drawings, finds encouragement when he sees his sister collecting and displaying his drawings. She tells him a vase he drew looks "vase-ish" and her words inspire him to think "ish-ly" and let his creative juices flow. Like *The Dot*, *Ish* celebrates a child's artistic expression and provides a lesson about how hurtful words can be.

Scarry, Richard. *Cars and Trucks and Things That Go*. New York: Random House, 1974.
This book is probably more suited to boys in kindergarten and grade one, although older boys might still enjoy it. The book shows a wide range of animals of both sexes engaging in all kinds of tasks. Names like Officer Flossie and Mistress Mouse are a little hard to take, but how many children's books show female police officers and mechanics? The gender balance is especially notable given the book's 1974 publication date.

Seuss, Dr. *My Many Colored Days*. New York: Random House Books, 1996.

> For various reasons, emotional expression can be difficult for boys. This book demonstrates that people have a range of emotions from "happy pink" to "mad and loud" black. It gives children a way to express their emotions by relating them to colours, while reassuring them that it is okay to be sad or angry because they will go back to being themselves again in due time.

Shaw, Mary and Chuck Temple. *Brady Brady and the Ballpark Bark*. Waterloo: Brady Brady Inc., 2007.

> This is just one title in a series featuring a male protagonist who faces challenges with great aplomb. He has a sense of justice and clearly cares for his friends. The stories all have a sports theme to which both boys and girls can relate.

Watt, Mélanie. *Scaredy Squirrel*. Toronto: Kids Can Press Ltd., 2006.

> This is the first title in a series about a male squirrel who is afraid to leave his tree and goes overboard with precautions whenever he does venture out. The books in this series are clever and funny. They offer a good counterbalance to the tough and brave male characters boys often see. Through the adventures of Scaredy Squirrel, kids learn that being scared is okay, they can overcome their fears, and the thing they were scared of might not be so scary after all.

Chapter Books

Blume, Judy. *Tales of a Fourth-Grade Nothing*. New York: Puffin Books, 1972.

> *Tales of a Fourth-Grade Nothing* is the first in Blume's "Fudge" series. The protagonist is Peter, a boy in fourth grade who is trying to deal with his mischievous younger brother. Peter is a very good role model for young boys and someone to whom all older siblings can relate. He is sensitive and caring, even when exasperated by his brother.

The series also wins points for its portrayal of fathers. Peter's father is very involved with his family. At one point he takes a sabbatical from his job, allowing Peter's mother to return to work. In a departure from most stories, the parents of Peter's best friend are divorced and the boy lives with his father, not his mother. She is not an entirely sympathetic figure, but a father with custody after a marriage breakdown is a refreshing change.

Gay, Marie-Louise and David Homel. *Travels with my Family.* Toronto: Groundwood Books, 2006.

The author of the *Stella* series, mentioned above, has collaborated with her husband on this selection of short tales about the parents of two boys who like to take their children "off the beaten path" when on vacation. The stories are funny, inventive and, like some of the others I have listed here, they include a positive portrayal of a father. The sequel, *On the Road Again*, sees the family travelling to France and is equally entertaining.

Greenburg, J.C. *Andrew Lost: On the Dog.* New York: Random House, 2002.

This title is the first in a series featuring boy inventor Andrew Dubble, his robot Thudd, and his cousin Judy. The three characters get shrunk to a size smaller than fleas by Andrew's Atom Sucker and end up exploring various environments up close. In the first book, they land on a dog and have to find their way out of its nose in an effort to escape. The situations can get a little yucky, but the writer deliberately avoids vulgar language. Rather, he takes advantage of his characters' predicaments to teach kids about science in an entertaining and creative way. Each book also contains facts and other resources about the subject matter discussed in that volume.

Lasky, Kathryn. *The Deadlies: Felix Takes the Stage*. New York: Scholastic Press, 2010.

This book, which launches a new series, tells the story of a family of brown recluse spiders, a variety of spider with very toxic venom. In the book, the family has to leave its home in a philharmonic hall in Los Angeles to escape the exterminators who are coming because of an accident involving young spider, Felix, and the orchestra's conductor. It is a lovely story that deftly weaves (pardon the pun) facts about many varieties of spiders, early New Englanders, and the city of Boston with a fictional tale that includes valuable life lessons, adventure, and suspense.

Felix, like many other male protagonists, is different from others of his species and wants to become an artist. A career in the arts would involve being seen—a definite no-no for Felix's reclusive mother Edith. Edith initially has reservations about her son's desire to explore, but in the end, she allows her son and daughters increased freedom. Edith is strong, smart and resourceful, as are her daughters, who rescue another spider from an attack by pirate spiders. Edith is also very accepting of her son's different nature.

Although there is no father character, he is acknowledged and missed. He is replaced to some degree by a male cat who accompanies Edith and her children on their journey—not that Edith couldn't manage on her own. Edith can sometimes seem overprotective. This trait could be misunderstood as a stereotype of the smothering mother, but is really justifiable given Edith's past experiences with exterminators and frightened humans.

Lindgren, Astrid. *Pippi Longstocking*. New York: Penguin Young Reader Group, 2005.

Pippi Longstocking is considered a classic character in children's literature, and for good reason. This first book is funny and the protagonist irrepressible. (Supporting characters lead more traditional lives.) Pippi gets herself into trouble sometimes and she certainly marches to the beat of her own drummer, most notably by avoiding school and any sort of formal education, but she is not a "brat" character like so many we see in kids' literature. She is a free spirit who offers children an escape and a different perspective on life. This book is fun for boys and girls to read.

Kline, Suzy. *Harry the Horrible in Room 2B*. New York: Puffin Books, 1988.

Although described as "horrible," lead character Harry is not nearly as bad as his name implies. He is a bright boy with a sometimes mischievous streak, but he is a good friend to his classmates. His schemes may break the rules but are usually carried out with good intentions. The kids in his peer group include boys and girls who can, at times, seem stereotypical, but are more often than not just typical kids. Some girls like bugs and science, some boys get scared, and both boys and girls find themselves tempted to follow Harry into adventure and misadventure.

McDonald, Megan. *Judy Moody*. Somerville. Candlewick Press, 2000.

This series of books features Judy Moody, a third-grade girl with ambitions to be a doctor. Although she may come off as a little abrasive at first, it quickly becomes apparent that she is a goodhearted child, especially in books like the second in the series—*Judy Moody Gets Famous*—where she anonymously fixes up dolls for young patients at the local hospital. Judy can be impatient with and jealous of her younger brother, but the rivalry in their relationship is something that most kids face in their everyday lives and would be glad to see documented in a book. The books have good male role models too, including Judy's male friends and her father, an active and involved parent.

Oppel, Kenneth. *A Bad Case of Ghosts*. Toronto: HarperCollins, 2010.
Originally published in 1994, this series of books (known as *Barnes and the Brains*) was reprinted in 2010. The three protagonists include a young boy named Giles and his friends, brother and sister Kevin and Tina, also known as the Quark geniuses. Both the Quark siblings and Giles have active and involved parents. The male characters are good role models, as are the females who have non-traditional roles: Giles' mother is a mathematician and Tina is an exceptionally intelligent young inventor whose contraptions are used to solve mysteries. Unfortunately, she is very harsh to her equally intelligent brother, but overall, the series offers good gender balance and great mystery stories.

Osborne, Mary Pope. *Hour of the Olympics*. New York: Random House, 1993.
This title is one of my favourites in the *Magic Tree House* series. The series features two siblings, Jack and Annie, who travel back in time to visit historically significant places. Jack is older and studious and Annie is an energetic and inquisitive girl. Although Annie is sometimes shown as more reckless than Jack, both children are equally involved in seeking adventure and in leading themselves out of misadventure. They clearly enjoy a healthy sibling relationship, with not a hint of condescension between the older boy and younger girl. Although he sometimes rolls his eyes at her, Jack respects his sister, treats her as his equal, and never takes on the role of protector.

I have selected this particular title because it involves a trip to ancient Greece, where the children get a lesson in gender equality when they discover that girls in that era were not allowed to go to school, attend the Olympic games, or act in plays. Titles build on each other, so it is best to read this series in order.

Paulsen, Gary. *Mudshark*. New York: Random House, 2009.

This book is intended for a slightly older audience than the one I am discussing here, but it is a great story to read aloud. The book is funny and includes a wonderful male protagonist. He is respectful of adults and sensitive to others, including his triplet toddler sisters. He is also extremely intelligent, a trait that his friends find cool, not nerdy.

Sharmat, Marjorie Weinman. *Nate the Great and the Monster Mess*. New York: Dell Yearling, 1999.

Although the name, *Nate the Great*, implies arrogance, the protagonist is really a nice young boy with a knack for solving mysteries. Nate has both male and female friends and has a reasoned approach to the problems he solves. The only issue with this series is that the father seems to be a non-entity. Parents should also note that the adventures are rather tame and would appeal more to younger readers.

Television

In selecting television shows for this list I was looking for good male role models and some degree of balance between male and female characters. I was also hoping to find programs that were entertaining, included some action, and had little or no violence. Finding all of these traits in one show was very difficult, so some of the shows included here do have violence. Others are just plain funny and entertaining for everyone. This list is sorted by title.

Arthur, PBS Kids, DVD.

Suited to children in the kindergarten age range, *Arthur* includes a mixture of male and female characters who get along and play well together, with no gender-based teasing or rivalry. Even more important, boys play without the aggression and competitiveness that characterize so many other shows. Because this show is heavy on lessons, people make mistakes but they also learn from them. This program also has very positive messages about parenting, as fathers are present and involved in their families. (The similarly themed *Franklin the Turtle* is also a good show, but suited more to viewers of a younger age than the one I am discussing here.)

Curious George, PBS Kids, DVD.

Based on the popular book series, the televised version of *Curious George* has the same attributes as the books. It also adds an educational element through its segments with real children exploring the themes discussed in the show. Recent episodes have talked about highly relevant issues like solar power, recycling, and composting.

Grossology, YTV, Nickelodeon Canada.

I mentioned this show in an earlier chapter. Studies have shown that many boys like action and enjoy seeing characters overcome challenges. *Grossology* fits the bill on both counts. There is action without violence. Characters use their brains and some pretty cool gadgets to solve mysteries. There is humour and an equal balance between older sister Abby and younger brother Ty. The siblings' parents are also involved with their children, although they are a tad "uncool." Abby can be a bit silly at times—gushing over animals and boys—but overall she is depicted as a smart and confident girl who likes science. Males are also strong characters, save for the somewhat ridiculous Director. Some of the language and situations are a bit crass but not entirely out of place in a program about human gas, vomit, and other yucky things.

Inspector Gadget, Teletoon Retro.

This show gets repetitive after a while, but with his gadgets and naiveté, Inspector Gadget will amuse most kids. He is accompanied on his adventures by his niece, a bright and courageous young girl.

Mighty Machines, Treehouse, TVO, DVD.

I have relied on this show countless times to occupy my children while I tend to things like dinner or cleaning. Its production values are not fantastic, but kids love this show. *Mighty Machines*, produced in Canada, features footage of real machines working, with each machine "talking" about the tasks it performs in language kids can understand. Machines are a mix of both sexes. While adults may find the accents used by the voice actors to be a little over-the-top, they are quite entertaining to children. Subjects covered by the series include mining, farming, waste collection and disposal, public transit, construction machines, and fire trucks and other rescue vehicles.

Scooby-Doo, Where Are You? and *The Scooby-Doo Show*, Teletoon Retro, Boomerang, DVD.

Originally produced in the 1960s and 1970s, these programs show their age in some respects, especially in their occasional ethnic stereotypes. Still, they can be considered progressive for including two female main characters as equal mystery-solving partners. Shaggy is not an ideal role model, but unlike the case with many cartoons of today, he is not positioned as a complete loser in comparison to group leader Fred—a character who is also shown running in fear from the villains the gang encounters in each episode. Overall, these are fun shows for kids that do not trade on gender stereotypes.

Parents should note that one of the newer incarnations of this show, *What's New Scooby-Doo*, is not quite as forward-thinking. Daphne is dumbed down in the modernized version and Fred seems to have developed a paternalistic instinct to protect the "girls," as he frequently calls Daphne and Velma.

Super Friends, Teletoon Retro, DVD.

> For young boys needing a superhero fix and parents seeking a gentler superhero story, this 1970s series might fit the bill. There is very little violence and a fair amount of action as Superman, Batman, Wonder Woman, and the other heroes save the day. The show is pretty campy and, like *Scooby-Doo, Where Are You,* includes some ethnic stereotypes that were common in that day and age, but it may appeal to youngsters who have not yet been exposed to the extreme violence of *Justice League* and *Justice League Unlimited.* (I would recommend the "classic" *Spider-Man* as well, but its availability seems to be limited to Teletoon Retro in Canada.)

Movies

This list contains films that achieve some degree of gender balance or, failing that, are notable for an absence of gender issues. Because action and excitement are important to boys but are usually manifested as violence, I found it impossible to avoid violence altogether, but I have indicated which of these films contain violent scenes.

A Bug's Life, Disney/Pixar, 1998.

> This is one of the rare films that achieves gender balance, teaches some valuable lessons, and still manages to entertain. Except for the evil grasshoppers, the other bugs are a combination of male and female characters. (That the "bad guys" are all guys is my only point of criticism in this film.) To help defend his colony against the grasshoppers, lead male Flick sets out to find "tough warrior bugs," but ends up with circus bugs who, thinking they are getting a new acting gig, decide to help Flick. Although it may go over the heads of young viewers, this emphasis on toughness provides a lesson—those who appear tough may not be, and those who appear meek are capable of great bravery.

There are many female characters in the cast, and males and females contribute equally to the resolution of the ants' problem. A couple of females even get to be heroes. There is also a funny sub-plot about a male ladybug continually being mistaken for a female. He later finds his "feminine side" and is happy about it. Note that there are some frightening scenes, so young children might have trouble with this film.

Everyone's Hero, Dan Krech Productions, 2006.

This film was reviewed harshly by critics and, to be honest, I had never heard of it before researching this book. Set in the 1930s, it is the story of a young boy who loves playing baseball but is not very good at it. He is picked on in sandlot games but becomes a hero when he finds and returns Babe Ruth's stolen lucky bat in time to help the New York Yankees win the World Series. The critics are right in saying that it is predictable with an ending that is difficult to believe. There are also a few anachronisms that may be obvious to parents but not as much to kids. Still, the movie has a sweetness to it and some funny moments that will appeal to children. The lead character is teased for his lack of skill with a bat, but he shows confidence in himself when he chooses to swing at the ball rather than just take his pitches and draw a walk when he is at the plate. It also includes two very likeable father characters who love and show affection for their children.

The Incredibles, Disney/Pixar, 2004.

This story of a family of superheroes in hiding has some very violent moments, and the villain is killed, albeit off-screen. Still, there are plenty of strong females and a father who is devoted to his family. The characters of Mirage and Frozone veer into stereotype territory, but overall the film offers a good degree of gender balance and a great story. The family does have one stereotypical aspect to it—Mom stays home while Dad goes to work. This attempt to look like a so-called normal family is more likely a result of their desire to keep their identities a secret than a sign of gender imbalance, although kids may not grasp that nuance.

Kiki's Delivery Service, Studio Ghibli, 1989.

This critically acclaimed Japanese film tells the story of a young witch who must leave home to begin her training. It is a traditional coming of age story, but with some twists that make it decidedly different from North American films. The protagonist is a girl and, although a bit giddy, she is strong, adventurous, resourceful, and independent. She has a close relationship with both of her parents, but in their absence finds two women to help her overcome the challenges she faces. She also proves herself a hero as she rescues her friend when he is in dire need of help.

The pace may be a little slow for some viewers, but the animation and storytelling are excellent.

Star Wars: The Clone Wars, Lucasfilm, 2008.

I had reservations about recommending this film because of the violence. I decided to include it because it has the type of "good versus evil" storyline that appeals to a lot of boys. Unlike many others in this genre, *Clone Wars* also includes strong characters of both sexes. The males are saddled to some degree with the warrior ethic of emotional detachment, but are good people at heart.

Although sexualized in appearance, Ahsoka, Amidala, and Ventress are all strong women who can take care of themselves. This film is also notable for allowing a female to defend herself and bring about a successful conclusion to her mission.

Because of the frequent battle scenes, parents may deem the violence too intense for young viewers. Common Sense Media rates it as suitable for ages eight and up.

(I excluded the *Clone Wars* television program from my list of recommendations for TV shows because of its more intense violence. Season 1 of the TV show is much like the film, but in Season 2 the show takes a darker turn with the inclusion of many bounty hunter characters. Dead clone soldiers are shown, murder is threatened in a sometimes graphic fashion, and the violence seems more gratuitous. Although only two episodes of Season 3 had aired before I wrote this book, it appears that the violence and mature themes continue in newer episodes.)

Shaun the Sheep, Aardman, 2007.

This collection of short films is made by the team behind the more well-known *Wallace & Gromit* cartoons and the movie *Chicken Run*. There is virtually no dialogue in these films that feature a somewhat dim farmer and his mischievous farm animals. Kids will laugh out loud at the antics of Shaun and the other animals.

Wallace & Gromit in Three Amazing Adventures, Aardman, 1990.

Along with the collection of short films called *Cracking Contraptions*, these films are fun for adults and children alike. Wallace is an inventor of sorts. When he gets into trouble, his dog Gromit saves the day.

Video Games

As with films and television, I was looking for games that entertain without too much violence or too many gender stereotypes.

My Sims: Agents, Electronic Arts, 2009

The MySims series allows children to create a virtual character and lead that character through a simulated life. In the *Agents* version, a child creates an agent who helps protect an imaginary city from a thief while following clues to identify and capture the villain. Along the way, agents meet people who get stored in their contacts list and play skill-testing games that earn them money. With their earnings, they can upgrade and decorate their houses. (I would prefer a game that does not promote shopping, but that is one of the realities of the Sims series.)

Agents can be male or female and the town includes characters of both sexes, including a male mayor and female police officer. Overall this is a fun and very balanced game, save for the programming glitch that causes female agents to be referred to as "Sir." Parents should note that this game appears to be highly addictive, so limits on its use may be necessary. Children also need to be able to read at a high level, making this game more suited to seven- and eight-year-olds.

Mario Kart, Nintendo, 2008

The *Mario* titles are not always gender-sensitive, but this game comes close. The females are very feminine in appearance, but they get to race as equals to the males. Unlike some of the other *Mario* games, there is no "mild cartoon violence," only "comic mischief." In promotional materials, Peach is featured alongside main characters Mario and Luigi, which promotes gender balance, to some degree.

This title stands in contrast to *New Super Mario Brothers* and *Mario & Luigi: Bowser's Inside Story*. In both of these games, Princess Peach is in need of rescue.

References

Research

Almon, Joan. "The Vital Role of Play in Childhood," in *All Work and No Play: How Educational Reforms are Harming Our Preschoolers*. ed. Sharna Olfman (Santa Barbara: Greenwood Publishing Group, 2003), 17-42.

Anderson, David A. and Mykol Hamilton "Gender role stereotyping of parents in children's picture books: the invisible father." *Sex Roles* 52, no. 3-4 (2005): 145-151.

Barlett, Chris et al. "Action figures and men." *Sex Roles* 53, no. 11-12 (2005): 877-885.

Bernthal, Matthew. "How Viewing Professional Wrestling May Affect Children." *The Sport Journal*. 6, no. 3 (2003), accessed on March 28, 2010, http://www.thesportjournal.org/article/effect-professional-wrestling-viewership-children.

Blakemore, Judith E. Owen and Renee E. Centers. "Characteristics of boys' and girls' toys." *Sex Roles* 53, no. 9-10 (2005): 619-633.

Brescoll, Victoria L. and Eric Luis Uhlmann. "Attitudes Toward Traditional and Nontraditional Parents." *Psychology of Women Quarterly* 29, no. 4 (2005): 436-445.

Cherney, Isabelle D. and Kamala London. "Gender-linked differences in the toys, television shows, computer games, and outdoor activities of 5- to 13-year-old children." *Sex Roles.* 54, no. 9-10 (2006): 717-726.

Children Now. *Boys to Men: Media Messages About Masculinity.* Oakland: Children Now, 2000.

Cloud, John. "Never Too Buff." *Time,* April 24, 2000.

Corson, Patricia Westmoreland and Arnold E. Andersen. "Body Image Issues Among Boys and Men," in *Body Image: A Handbook of Theory, Research, and Clinical Practice.* New York: The Guilford Press, 2002, 192-199.

Daniels, Les. *Superman: The Complete History.* San Francisco: Chronicle Books, 1998.

Dunnigan, James F. *How to Make War: A Comprehensive Guide to Modern Warfare in the Twenty-First Century,* 4th ed. New York: HarperCollins,Quill, 2003.

Durham, M. Gigi. *The Lolita Effect: The Media Sexualization of Young Girls and What We Can Do About It.* Woodstock: Overlook Press, 2008.

Etcoff, Nancy. *Survival of the Prettiest.* New York: Doubleday, 1999.

Fine, Cordelia. *Delusions of Gender.* New York: W.W. Norton & Company, 2010.

Götz, Maya et al. *Girls and Boys and Television: A few reminders for more gender sensitivity in children's TV*. Munich: International Central Institute for Youth and Educational Television, 2008.

Graddol, David and Joan Swann. *Gender voices*. Oxford: Basil Blackwell Ltd., 1989.

Hall, Joseph. "Young children feel the weight of body image." *The Toronto Star*. August 27, 2009.

Hamilton, Mykol C. "Gender stereotyping and under-representation of female characters in 200 popular children's picture books: a twenty-first century update." *Sex Roles* 55, no. 11-12 (2006): 757-765.

Hardin, Marie and Jennifer D. Greer. "The influence of gender-role socialization, media use and sports participation on perceptions of gender-appropriate sports." *Journal of Sports Behavior* 32 (June 1, 2009).

Hobbes, Nicholas. *Essential Militaria*. Toronto: McArthur & Company, 2004.

Holland, Penny. *We don't play with guns here: War, weapon and superhero play in the early years*. Berkshire: Open University Press, 2003.

Homer. *The Iliad*. Translated by Samuel Butler. 1898. Reprint, London: Arcturus Publishing, 2009.

Holland, Jack. *Misogyny: The World's Oldest Prejudice*. New York: Carroll & Graf Publishers, 2006.

Jordan, Ellen. (1995) "Fighting Boys and Fantasy Play: the construction of masculinity in the early years of school." *Gender and Education* 7, no. 1, (1995): 69-86.

Josephson, Wendy L. *Television Violence: A Review of the Effects on Children At Different Ages*. Ottawa: Department of Canadian Heritage, 1995. Reprinted with permission by Media Awareness Network http://www.media-awareness.ca/english/resources/research_documents/reports/violence/tv_violence_child.cfm.

Jule, Allyson. *A Beginner's Guide to Language and Gender*. Cleveden: Multilingual Matters, 2008.

Kindlon, Dan and Michael Thompson. *Raising Cain: Protecting the Emotional Life of Boys*. New York: Random House, 2000.

Lee, Christina and R. Glynn Owens. *The psychology of men's health*. Buckingham: Open University Press, 2002.

Levant, Ronald F. "Men and Masculinity," in Vol. 2 of *Encyclopedia of Women and Gender: Sex Similarities and Differences and the Impact of Society on Gender*. ed. Judith Worrell. (San Diego: Academic Press, 2001), 717-727.

Machiavelli, Niccolo. *The Art of War*. 1521. Translated by Neal Wood. Cambridge, MA: Da Capo Press, 2001.

Madrid, Mike. *The Supergirls: Fashion, feminism, fantasy and the history of comic book heroines*. Minneapolis: Exterminating Angel Press, 2009.

Media Awareness Network. *TV Dads: Backgrounder for Teachers*. accessed on May 15, 2010 http://www.media-awareness.ca/english/resources/educational/teaching_backgrounders/stereotyping/tv_dads_backgrounder.cfm.

Messner, Mike et al. *Boys to Men: Sports Media Messages About Masculinity*. Oakland: Children Now, 1999.

Nathanson, Paul and Katherine K. Young. *Spreading Misandry: The Teaching of Contempt for Men in Popular Culture*. Montréal: McGill-Queen's University Press, 2001.

National Research Council. *Human Behaviour in Military Contexts*. Edited by James J. Blascovich and Christine R. Hartel. Washington, DC: The National Academies Press, 2008.

Oleck, Joan. "Gender Stereotypes Still Persist in Films." *School Library Journal*, November 3, 2006, accessed Dec. 1, 2009 http://www.schoollibraryjournal.com/article/CA6387189.html.

Ormsby, Mary and Leslie Scrivener. "What a 9-Year-Old Thinks." *Toronto Star*, January 31, 2010.

Perkins, Dave. "Milquetoast Blue Jays could use a little moxie." *Toronto Star*. August 21, 2009.

Pike, Jennifer and Nancy A. Jennings. "The effects of commercials on children's perception of gender appropriate toy use." *Sex Roles* 52, no. 1-2 (2005): 83-91.

Pollack, William. *Real Boys: Rescuing Our Sons from the Myths of Boyhood*. New York: Random House, 1998.

Pope, Harrison et al. *The Adonis Complex*. New York: Touchstone, 2000.

Quinn, Susan M. Flannery. "The depictions of fathers and children in best-selling picture books in the United States: a hybrid semiotic analysis." *Fathering*. March 22, 2009.

Ryan, Erin. "Dora the Explorer: Giving Power to Preschoolers, Girls, and Latinas" Paper presented at the annual meeting of the Association for Education in Journalism and Mass Communication, The Renaissance, Washington, DC, August 8, 2007.

Sacks, Glenn and Richard Samglick. "Advertisers: Men Are Not Idiots." *Advertising Age*, April 14, 2008.

Silverstein, Olga and Beth Rashbaum. *The Courage to Raise Good Men*. New York: Penguin Books, 1994.

Smith, Dr. Stacy L. and Cooke, Crystal Allene. *Gender Stereotypes: An Analysis of Popular Films and TV*. Los Angeles: Geena Davis Institute on Gender in Media, 2008.

Smolak, Linda "Body Image Development in Children," in *Body Image: A Handbook of Theory, Research, and Clinical Practice*. New York: The Guilford Press, 2002, 66-68.

Spettigue, Wendy and Katherine A. Henderson. "Eating Disorders and the Role of the Media," *The Canadian Child and Adolescent Psychiatry Review*, 13, no. 1 (2004): 16-19.

Statius, Publius Papinius. *The Achilleid*, http://www.theoi.com/Text/StatiusAchilleid1A.html, Accessed on March 28, 2010.

Sun, Chyng. *Mickey Mouse Monopoly: Disney, Childhood & Corporate Power*. Transcript. Northampton, MA: Media Education Foundation, 2001.

Swann, Joan. *Girls, Boys and Language*. Oxford: Blackwell Publishers, 1992.

Tiggeman, Marika. "Media Influences on Body Image Development," in *Body Image: A Handbook of Theory, Research, and Clinical Practice*. New York: The Guilford Press, 2002. 91-98.

U.S. Census Bureau. "Facts for Features: Unmarried and Single Americans Week Sept. 20-26, 2009." *U.S. Census Bureau News*, July 21, 2009.

Ven Petten, Vanessa. "How to Win the Gender War: Sexism and Teens." *Radical Parenting*, May, 2009. http://www.radicalparenting. com/2009/05/12/how-to-win-the-gender-war-sexism-and-teens-teen-article/.

Ward, L. Monique and Allison Caruthers. "Media Influences," in Vol. 2 of *Encyclopedia of Women and Gender: Sex Similarities and Differences and the Impact of Society on Gender.* ed. Judith Worrell. (San Diego: Academic Press, 2001), 687-701.

Witt, Susan D. (1997). "Parental influence on children's socialization to gender roles." *Adolescence.* 32, no. 126 (1997): 253-260.

Wood, Eileen, Serge Desmarais and Sara Gugula. "The impact of parenting experience on gender stereotyped toy play of children." *Sex Roles* 47, no. 1-2 (2002): 39-49.

Children's Books

Barrett, Judy. *Cloudy with a Chance of Meatballs.* New York: Simon and Schuster Children's Publishing, 1978.

Beecroft, Simon. *Star Wars, The Clone Wars: Anakin In Action.* New York: DK Publishing, 2008.

Bolger, Kevin. *Sir Fartsalot Hunts the Booger.* New York: Penguin, 2008.

Brown, Margaret Wise. *Goodnight Moon.* New York: Harper Collins, 1947.

Cottringer, Anne. *Eliot Jones, Midnight Superhero*. Toronto: Scholastic Canada, 2008.

Cowell, Cressida. *How to Train Your Dragon*. London: Hachette Children's Books, 2003.

Dahl, Roald. *Fantastic Mr. Fox*. New York: Puffin Books, 2007.

Falconer, Ian. *Olivia*. New York: Simon and Schuster Children's Publishing, 2000.

Falconer, Ian. *Olivia Saves the Circus*. New York: Simon and Schuster Children's Publishing, 2001.

Falconer, Ian. *Olivia Forms a Band*. New York: Simon and Schuster Children's Publishing, 2006.

Greenburg, J.C. *Andrew Lost: On the Dog*. New York: Random House, 2002.

Greenburg, J.C. *Andrew Lost: In the Bathroom*. New York: Random House, 2002.

Hall, Jason. *Justice League: The Animated Series Guide*. New York: DK Publishing, 2004.

Hutchins, Hazel and Gail Herbert. *Mattland*. Toronto: Annick Press, 2008.

Keats, Ezra Jack. *Snowy Day*. New York: Viking Press, 1962.

Kline, Suzy. *Horrible Harry and the Dead Letters*. New York: Viking, 2008.

Kline, Suzy. *Horrible Harry and the Mud Gremlins*. New York: Puffin Books, 2003.

Kline, Suzy. *Horrible Harry Bugs the Three Bears*. New York: Viking, 2008.

Kline, Suzy. *Horrible Harry Cracks the Code*. New York: Puffin Books, 2007.

Kline, Suzy. *Horrible Harry in Room 2B*. New York: Puffin Books, 1988.

Kotzwinkle, William and Glenn Murray. *Walter the Farting Dog*. Berkeley: Frog Books, 2001.

Larry, H.I. *Zac Power: Deep Waters*. Toronto: Scholastic Canada, 2007.

Larry, H.I. *Zac Power: Frozen Fear*. Toronto: Scholastic Canada, 2006.

Larry, H.I. *Zac Power: Poison Island*. Toronto: Scholastic Canada, 2007.

Lasky, Kathryn. *The Deadlies: Felix Takes the Stage*. New York: Scholastic Press, 2010.

Leaf, Munro. *The Story of Ferdinand*. New York: Puffin, 1936.

Mason, Simon. *The Quigleys in a Spin*. New York: Random House, 2006.

McDonald, Megan. *Judy Moody*. Somerville, MA: Candlewick Press, 2000.

McDonald, Megan. *Judy Moody Gets Famous*. Somerville, MA: Candlewick Press, 2001.

McDonald, Megan. *Judy Moody & Stink: The Mad, Mad, Mad, Mad Treasure Hunt.* Somerville, MA: Candlewick Press, 2009.

McDonald, Megan. *Stink and the Great Guinea Pig Express.* Somerville, MA: Candlewick Press, 2008.

McDonald, Megan. *Stink and the Incredible Super-Galactic Jawbreaker.* Somerville, MA: Candlewick Press, 2006.

McDonald, Megan. *Stink and the World's Worst Super-Stinky Sneakers.* Somerville, MA: Candlewick Press, 2007.

Munsch, Robert. *Andrew's Loose Tooth.* Toronto: Scholastic Canada, 1998.

Munsch, Robert. *Just One Goal.* Toronto: Scholastic Canada, 2008.

Munsch, Robert. *Look At Me.* Toronto: Scholastic Canada, 2008.

Munsch, Robert. *Love You Forever.* Toronto: Firefly, 1995.

Munsch, Robert. *Much More Munsch.* Toronto: Scholastic Canada, 2007.

Munsch, Robert and Askar, Saoussan. *Munschworks 4.* Toronto: Annick Press, 2002.

Munsch, Robert. *The Paper Bag Princess.* Toronto: Annick Press, 1980.

Munsch, Robert. *The Sandcastle Contest.* Toronto: Scholastic Canada, 2005.

Oppel, Kenneth. *A Bad Case of Ghosts.* Toronto: Scholastic Canada, 1993. Reprinted. Toronto: HarperCollins, 2010.

Oppel, Kenneth. *A Crazy Case of Robots*. Toronto: Scholastic Canada, 1994. Reprinted. Toronto: HarperCollins, 2010.

Oppel, Kenneth. *A Strange Case of Magic*. Toronto: Scholastic Canada, 1994. Reprinted. Toronto: HarperCollins, 2010.

Oppel, Kenneth. *A Weird Case of Super-Goo*. Toronto: Scholastic Canada, 1996. Reprinted. Toronto: HarperCollins, 2010.

Osborne, Mary Pope. *Magic Tree House #2: The Knight at Dawn*. New York: Random House, 1993.

Osborne, Mary Pope. *Magic Tree House #3: Mummies in the Morning*. New York: Random House, 1993.

Osborne, Mary Pope. *Magic Tree House #4: Pirates Past Noon*. New York: Random House, 1994.

Osborne, Mary Pope. *Magic Tree House #5: Night of the Ninjas*. New York: Random House, 1995.

Osborne, Mary Pope. *Magic Tree House #13: Vacation Under the Volcano*. New York: Random House, 1998.

Osborne, Mary Pope. *Magic Tree House #16: Hour of the Olympics*. New York: Random House, 1998.

Paulsen, Gary. *Mudshark*. New York: Random House, 2009.

Penn, Audrey. *The Kissing Hand*. Terre Haute, IN: Tanglewood Press, 1993.

Perez, Monica. *Curious George Plants a Tree*. New York: Houghton Mifflin, 2009.

Pilkey, Dav. *Captain Underpants and the Invasion of the Incredibly Naughty Cafeteria Ladies from Outer Space (and the Subsequent Assault of the Equally Evil Lunchroom Zombie Nerds)*. New York: Scholastic, 1999.

Pilkey, Dav. *Captain Underpants and the Perilous Plot of Professor Poopypants*. New York: Scholastic, 2000.

Pilkey, Dav. *Captain Underpants and the Wrath of the Wicked Wedgie Woman*. New York: Scholastic, 2001.

Rey, Margaret and H.A. *A Treasury of Curious George*. New York: Houghton Mifflin, 2004.

Reynolds, Peter H. *Ish*. Somerville, MA: Candlewick Press, 2004.

Reynolds, Peter H. *The Dot*. Somerville, MA: Candlewick Press, 2003.

Scarry, Richard. *Cars and Trucks and Things That Go*. New York: Random House, 1974.

Scieszka, Jon. *DaWild, DaCrazy, DaVinci*. New York: Puffin Books, 2004.

Scieszka, Jon. *Knights of the Kitchen Table*. New York: Puffin Books, 1991.

Scieszka, Jon. *Tut Tut*. New York: Puffin Books, 1996.

Scott, Heather. *Star Wars, The Clone Wars: Yoda In Action*. New York: DK Publishing, 2009.

Sendak., Maurice. *Where the Wild Things Are*. New York: Harper Collins, 1963.

Seuss, Dr. *The Cat in the Hat.* New York: Random House Books, 1957.

Seuss, Dr. *My Many Colored Days.* New York: Random House Books, 1996.

Sharmat, Marjorie Weinman. *Nate the Great and the Big Sniff.* New York: Random House, Delacorte Press, 2001.

Sharmat, Marjorie Weinman. *Nate the Great and the Lost List.* New York: Random House, Yearling, 1975.

Sharmat, Marjorie Weinman. *Nate the Great and the Monster Mess.* New York: Random House, Dell Yearling, 1999.

Sharmat, Marjorie Weinman. *Nate the Great on the Owl Express.* New York: Random House, Delacorte Press, 2003.

Sharmat, Marjorie Weinman. *Nate the Great: San Francisco Detective.* New York: Random House, Dell Yearling, 2000.

Shaw, Mary and Chuck Temple. *Brady Brady and the Ballpark Bark.* Waterloo: Brady Brady Inc., 2007.

Stilton, Geronimo. *A Cheese-Colored Camper.* New York: Scholastic, 2000.

Stilton, Geronimo. *A Very Merry Christmas.* New York: Scholastic, 2007.

Stilton, Geronimo. *Geronimo Stilton, Secret Agent.* New York: Scholastic, 2007.

Stilton, Geronimo. *Geronimo's Valentine.* New York: Scholastic, 2009.

Stilton, Geronimo. *My Name Is Stilton, Geronimo Stilton*: New York. Scholastic, 2000.

Stilton, Geronimo. *The Kingdom of Fantasy*. Toronto: Scholastic Canada, 2009.

Stilton, Geronimo. *The Race Across America*. New York: Scholastic, 2009.

Stilton, Geronimo. *Watch Your Whiskers, Stilton*. New York: Scholastic, 2001.

Teitelbaum, Michael. *The Story of Spider-Man*. New York: DK Publishing, 2001.

Watt, Mélanie. *Scaredy Squirrel*. Toronto: Kids Can Press, 2006.

Watt, Mélanie. *Scaredy Squirrel makes a friend*. Toronto: Kids Can Press, 2007.

Watt, Mélanie. *Scaredy Squirrel at the beach*. Toronto: Kids Can Press, 2008.

West, Tracey. *The Battle Brawlers*. New York: Scholastic, 2009.

West, Tracey. *The Party Crashers*. New York: Scholastic, 2009.

Music

Jacob, Danny. "My Nemesis." *Phineas and Ferb: Songs From the Hit Disney TV Series*. Walt Disney Records, 2009.

Dr. Doofenshmirtz. "My Goody Two-Shoes Brother." *Phineas and Ferb: Songs From the Hit Disney TV Series*. Walt Disney Records, 2009.

Various Artists. *SpongeBob's Greatest Hits.* Viacom International Ltd., 2009.

Wyckoff, Robbie. "He's A Bully." *Phineas and Ferb: Songs From the Hit Disney TV Series.* Walt Disney Records, 2009.

Online Resources

"Agents of Success," accessed October 16, 2010, http://goliath.ecnext.com/coms2/gi_0199-6892323/Agents-of-success-while-it.html

"Army Master Resilience Training course provides valued instruction," accessed August 15, 2010, http://www.army.mil/-news/2010/03/29/36520-army-master-resilience-training-course-provides-valued-instruction/.

"Bakugan Battle Brawlers Cast and Crew," accessed March 16, 2010, http://www.tv.com/bakugan-battle-brawlers/show/75192/cast.html.

Biography of Steve Reeves, accessed March 14, 2010, http://www.stevereeves.com/bio-bodybuilder.asp.

"Books That Guys Read," Guys Read, accessed August 2009. http://www.guysread.com/books/.

Boys' Make Believe page on Chapters/Indigo site, accessed July 11, 2010. http://www.chapters.indigo.ca/toys/Boys/606324-750072-750074-700014-606329-cat.html.

Boys' Role Play page on Toys R Us site, accessed May 23, 2010. http://www.toysrus.ca/category/index.jsp?categoryId=4192048&cp=4192048&clickid=leftnav_cat_txt.

Canadian Sports Hall of Fame, Honoured Members—Doug Flutie, accessed on August 28, 2010, http://cshof.ca/accessible/hm_profile.php?i=489.

Cohn, Bob. "Clarion's Hoggard piques NFL interest despite his size," Pittsburgh Tribune-Review, August 22, 2010, accessed August 28, 2010, http://www.pittsburghlive.com/x/pittsburghtrib/sports/college/s_695947.html.

Columbia Pictures. *Cloudy with a Chance of Meatballs* page, accessed March 16, 2010, http://www.cloudywithachanceofmeatballs.com/.

Common Sense Media, "Boys and Body Image Tips," *Common Sense Media*, accessed August 27, 2009, http://www.commonsensemedia.org/boys-and-body-image-tips.

Dav's Books, accessed March 16, 2010, http://www.pilkey.com/bookview.php?id=19.

Girls' Make Believe page on Chapters/Indigo Site, accessed July 11, 2010, http://www.chapters.indigo.ca/toys/Girls/606324-750072-750074-700014-606330-cat.html .

Girls' Role Play page on Toys R Us site, accessed March 23, 2010. http://www.toysrus.ca/category/index.jsp?categoryId=4192046&cp=4192046&clickid=leftnav_cat_txt.

Hulk Hogan biography, *HulkHogan.net*, accessed October 17, 2010, http://hulkhogan.net/hulk-hogan-biography/hulk-hogan-personal-biography?view=item.

"Hulk Hogan, on Witness Stand, Tells of Steroid Use in Wrestling," *New York Times Archives*, July 15, 1994, http://www.nytimes.

com/1994/07/15/nyregion/hulk-hogan-on-witness-stand-tells-of-steroid-use-in-wrestling.html

Laskaris, Sam, "Amestoy Reaches Great Heights Despite Small Stature," *Hockey Now, Ontario Edition*, accessed August 28, 2010, http://www.ontariohockey.com/story/25/Junior%20A%20Report/4958/Amestoy_Reaches_Great_Heights_Despite_Small_Stature.aspx.

Lego Skrall character description, Lego Group, accessed August 15, 2010, http://bionicle.lego.com/en-us/story/bios/glatorian/Skrall.aspx.

Messner, Michael, "Dropping the Ball on Covering Women's Sports," *The Huffington Post*, June 3, 2010, accessed August 28, 2010. http://www.huffingtonpost.com/michael-messner/dropping-the-ball-on-cove_b_599912.html.

Miss Corolle product page, accessed April 27, 2010,http://www.corolle.com/us/catalogue/misscorolle.php5#intro.

"On-Air Personalities" *MLB.com,* accessed on August 28, 2010. http://mlb.mlb.com/network/personalities/.

"Mother's Day ... by the numbers" Statistics Canada, accessed May 29, 2010, http://www42.statcan.ca/smr08/2006/smr08_047_2006-eng.htm.

Nerf N-Strike page, Hasbro Toys, accessed February 15, 2010, http://www.hasbro.com/nerf/n-strike/shop/details.cfm?guid=940BFD86-6D40-1014-8BF0-9EFBF894F9D4&product_id=22378.

Pixar Films, *Cars* character description pages, accessed March 16, 2010, http://www.pixar.com/featurefilms/cars/characters.html.

Pompei, Dan. "Corner McMillian thrives despite lack of ideal size" in *The Sporting News*, November 16, 1998, accessed on August 28, 2010 on http://findarticles.com/p/articles/mi_m1208/is_1998_Nov_16/ai_53256082/.

Purple Princess Cape, accessed March 16, 2010 http://www.chapters.indigo.ca/toys/Purple-Princess-Cape-Medium-Great/771877501456-item.html.

Red Adventure cape page, accessed March 16, 2010 http://www.chapters.indigo.ca/toys/Red-Adventure-Cape-Small-Great/771877542732-item.html.

"Rita Mae Brown Quotes," *Brainy Quotes*, Accessed August 28, 2010, http://www.brainyquote.com/quotes/authors/r/rita_mae_brown_2.html

Statius, Publius Papinius. *The Achilleid*, Cambridge, MA: Harvard University Press, 2003, accessed March 28, 2010, http://www.theoi.com/Text/StatiusAchilleid1A.html.

Teletoon, *Bakugan Battle Brawlers* page, accessed October 3, 2009, http://www.teletoon.com/teletoon3/teletoon.php?language=En&func=php|templates/show.php|../tv/bakugan/bakugan_en.xml&xVar= .

Teletoon, *Iron Man: Armored Adventures* page, accessed March 16, 2010, http://www.teletoon.com/teletoon3/teletoon.php?language=En&func=php|templates/show.php|../tv/ironManArmoredAdventures/ironManArmoredAdventures_en.xml&xVar=0.

Teletoon, *What's New Scooby-Doo* page, accessed March 16, 2010, http://www.teletoon.com/teletoon3/teletoon.php?language=En&func=php|templates/show.php|../tv/whatsNewScoobyDoo/whatsNewScoobyDoo_en.xml&xVar=0.

"TV Dads: Backgrounder for Teachers," Media Awareness Network, accessed May 24, 2009, http://www.media-awareness.ca/english/resources/educational/teaching_backgrounders/stereotyping/tv_dads_backgrounder.cfm.

UFC Action Figure Karo Parysian page on Toys R Us site, accessed August 28, 2010, http://www.toysrus.ca/product/index.jsp?productId=4277397&prodFindSrc=search.

Women's Sports Foundation, "Women Play Sports but Not on TV," *Women's Sports Foundation*, June 4, 2010, accessed on August 28, 2010. http://womenssportsfoundation.org/Content/Articles/Research/W/Women-play-sports-but-not-on-TV.aspx.

Yessie, Ryan. "Ryan Yessie's Top 50 for 2010: Part 2 – 11 to 30", *OHL Prospects* (blog), May 31, 2010, accessed August 28, 2010, http://ohlprospects.blogspot.com/2010/05/ryan-yessies-top-50-for-2010-part-2-11.html.

Video

Television

Arthur

"Francine's Split Decision," *Arthur*. Boston: WGBH, 2002.

"I'm a Poet," *Arthur*. Boston: WGBH, 1997.

"Muffy Goes Metropolitan," *Arthur*. Boston: WGBH, 2002.

"The Election," *Arthur*. Boston: WGBH, 2000.

"World Record," *Arthur*. Boston: WGBH, 2000.

"You Are Arthur," *Arthur*. Boston: WGBH, 2000.

Atomic Betty

"Big Top Betty," *Atomic Betty*. Vancouver: Atomic Cartoons, 2005.

"Bracelet Yourself, Part 1," *Atomic Betty*. Vancouver: Atomic Cartoons, 2005.

"Bracelet Yourself, Part 2," *Atomic Betty*. Vancouver: Atomic Cartoons, 2005.

"Dr. Cerebral and the Stupefactor Ray," *Atomic Betty*. Vancouver: Atomic Cartoons, 2005.

"Pop Goes the Maxx," *Atomic Betty*. Vancouver: Atomic Cartoons, 2005.

"Sleeping Like a Baby," *Atomic Betty*. Vancouver: Atomic Cartoons, 2005.

Bakugan Battle Brawlers

"A Duel in the Desert," *Bakugan Battle Brawlers*. Tokyo: TMS Entertainment, 2008.

"A Fish Called Tayghen," *Bakugan Battle Brawlers*. Tokyo: TMS Entertainment, 2008.

"A Perfect Match," *Bakugan Battle Brawlers*. Tokyo: TMS Entertainment, 2008.

"A Place Far From Home," *Bakugan Battle Brawlers*. Tokyo: TMS Entertainment, 2008.

"Alice Gets Schooled," *Bakugan Battle Brawlers*. Tokyo: TMS Entertainment, 2008.

"Bakugan Stall," *Bakugan Battle Brawlers*. Tokyo: TMS Entertainment, 2008.

"Dan's Last Stand," *Bakugan Battle Brawlers*. Tokyo: TMS Entertainment, 2008.

"Ground Control to Major Dan," *Bakugan Battle Brawlers*. Tokyo: TMS Entertainment, 2008.

"Home Sweet Home," *Bakugan Battle Brawlers*. Tokyo: TMS Entertainment, 2008.

"Just for the Shun of It," *Bakugan Battle Brawlers*. Tokyo: TMS Entertainment, 2008.

"Show Me What You've Got," *Bakugan Battle Brawlers*. Tokyo: TMS Entertainment, 2008.

"You're Going Down Clown," *Bakugan Battle Brawlers*. Tokyo: TMS Entertainment, 2008.

Ben 10

"Perfect Day," *Ben 10*. Burbank, CA: Cartoon Network Studios, 2007.

"Under Wraps," *Ben 10*. Burbank, CA: Cartoon Network Studios, 2007.

Ben 10: Alien Force

"All That Glitters," *Ben 10: Alien Force.* DVD. Burbank, CA: Cartoon Network Studios, 2008.

"Ben 10 Returns: Part 1," *Ben 10: Alien Force.* DVD. Burbank, CA: Cartoon Network Studios, 2008.

"Ben 10 Returns: Part 2," *Ben 10: Alien Force.* DVD. Burbank, CA: Cartoon Network Studios, 2008.

"Don't Fear the Repo," *Ben 10: Alien Force.* Burbank, CA: Cartoon Network Studios, 2009.

"Everybody Talks About the Weather," *Ben 10: Alien Force.* DVD. Burbank, CA: Cartoon Network Studios, 2008.

"Kevin's Big Score," *Ben 10: Alien Force.* DVD. Burbank, CA: Cartoon Network Studios, 2008.

"Pier Pressure," *Ben 10: Alien Force.* Burbank, CA: Cartoon Network Studios, 2008.

"Simple," *Ben 10: Alien Force.* Burbank, CA: Cartoon Network Studios, 2009.

"Single Handed," *Ben 10: Alien Force.* Burbank, CA: Cartoon Network Studios, 2009.

Chaotic

"Train Wreck," *Chaotic.* San Diego: Chaotic USA Entertainment Group, 2008.

"Trading Cards," *Chaotic*. San Diego: Chaotic USA Entertainment Group, 2008.

Chaotic: M'arrillian Invasion

"From the Deep, Part 1," *Chaotic:M'arillian Invasion*. San Diego: Chaotic USA Entertainment Group, 2009.

"From the Deep, Part 2," *Chaotic:M'arillian Invasion*. San Diego: Chaotic USA Entertainment Group, 2009.

Curious George

"A Monkey's Duckling," *Curious George*. Boston, MA: WGBH Educational Foundation, 2010.

"Camping with Hundley," *Curious George*. Boston, MA: WGBH Educational Foundation, 2007.

"Curious George and the Turbo Python 3000," *Curious George*. Boston, MA: WGBH Educational Foundation, 2007.

"Everything Old is New Again," *Curious George*. Boston, MA: WGBH Educational Foundation, 2008.

"Movie House Monkey," *Curious George*. Boston, MA: WGBH Educational Foundation, 2009.

"George Digs Worms," *Curious George*. Boston, MA: WGBH Educational Foundation, 2008.

"Juicy George," *Curious George*. Boston, MA: WGBH Educational Foundation, 2009.

"One in a Million Chameleon," *Curious George*. Boston, MA: WGBH Educational Foundation, 2010.

Grossology

"Go Fish," *Grossology*. Toronto: Nelvana Ltd., 2006.

"It's Gotta Be the Shoes," *Grossology*. Toronto: Nelvana Ltd., 2006.

"Lights Out," *Grossology*. Toronto: Nelvana Ltd., 2007.

"Yack Attack," *Grossology*. Toronto: Nelvana Ltd., 2007.

Hot Wheels Battle Force 5

"Axis of Evil, Part 1 and 2," *Hot Wheels Battle Force 5*. Toronto: Nelvana, 2009.

"Mag Wheels," *Hot Wheels Battle Force 5*. Toronto: Nelvana, 2009.

"Mobi 3.0," *Hot Wheels Battle Force 5*. Toronto: Nelvana, 2009.

"Starting Line," *Hot Wheels Battle Force 5*. Toronto: Nelvana, 2009.

Iron Man: Armored Adventures

"Fun with Lasers," *Iron Man: Armored Adventures*. Los Angeles: Marvel Animation, 2009.

"Man and Iron Man," *Iron Man: Armored Adventures*. Los Angeles: Marvel Animation, 2009.

Johnny Test

"Johnny vs. Bling-Bling Boy 3," *Johnny Test*. Toronto: Teletoon Productions, 2007.

"Johnny vs. Dukey," *Johnny Test*. Toronto: Teletoon Productions, 2007.

"Johnny X and the Attack of the Snowmen," *Johnny Test*. Toronto: Teletoon Productions, 2007.

"Stinkin' Johnny," *Johnny Test*. Toronto: Teletoon Productions, 2007.

Justice League

"In Blackest Night, Part 1 and 2" *Justice League*. DVD. Burbank, CA: Warner Brothers, 2003.

"Injustice for All, Part 1 and 2," *Justice League*. DVD. Burbank, CA: Warner Brothers, 2002.

"The Enemy Below, Part 1 and 2," *Justice League*. DVD. Burbank, CA: Warner Brothers, 2003.

"Paradise Lost, Part 1 and 2," *Justice League*. DVD. Burbank, CA: Warner Brothers, 2003.

"The Brave and the Bold, Part 1 and 2," *Justice League*. DVD. Burbank, CA: Warner Brothers, 2002.

"War World, Part 1 and 2," *Justice League*. DVD. Burbank, CA: Warner Brothers, 2003.

Justice League Unlimited

"For the Man Who Has Everything," *Justice League Unlimited*. DVD. Burbank, CA: Warner Brothers, 2004.

"The Greatest Story Never Told," *Justice League Unlimited*. DVD. Burbank, CA: Warner Brothers, 2004.

"The Return," *Justice League Unlimited*. DVD. Burbank, CA: Warner Brothers, 2004.

Mad Men

"The Fog," *Mad Men*. DVD. Vancouver: Lionsgate Television. 2010.

Mighty Machines

"All About Recycling," *Mighty Machines: Volume 9*. DVD. Montréal: Seville Pictures, 2005.

"At the Garbage Dump," *Mighty Machines: Volume 9*. DVD. Montréal: Seville Pictures, 2005.

"At the Sawmill," *Mighty Machines: Tremendous Tools*. DVD. Montréal: Seville Pictures, 2007.

"Building a Truck," *Mighty Machines: Volume 9*. DVD. Montréal: Seville Pictures, 2005.

"Deep Underground," *Mighty Machines: Tremendous Tools*. DVD. Montréal: Seville Pictures, 2007.

"On the Farm," *Mighty Machines: Tremendous Tools*. DVD. Montréal: Seville Pictures, 2007.

Penguins of Madagascar

"Penguiner Takes All," *Penguins of Madagascar*. Burbank, CA: Nickelodeon Animation, 2009.

"The Red Squirrel," *Penguins of Madagascar*. Burbank, CA: Nickelodeon Animation, 2010.

"Two Feet High and Rising," *Penguins of Madagascar*. Burbank, CA: Nickelodeon Animation, 2009.

Phineas and Ferb

"Bubble Boys," *Phineas and Ferb*. Los Angeles: Walt Disney Television Animation, 2009.

"Candace's Big Day," *Phineas and Ferb*. Los Angeles: Walt Disney Television Animation, 2010.

"Cheer Up Candace," *Phineas and Ferb*. Los Angeles: Walt Disney Television Animation, 2009.

"Does This Duckbill Make Me Look Fat?" *Phineas and Ferb*. Los Angeles: Walt Disney Television Animation, 2009.

"Finding Mary McGuffin," *Phineas and Ferb*. Los Angeles: Walt Disney Television Animation, 2009.

"Fireside Girl Jamboree," *Phineas and Ferb*. Los Angeles: Walt Disney Television Animation, 2009.

"Got Game," *Phineas and Ferb*. Los Angeles: Walt Disney Television Animation, 2008.

"Isabella and the Temple of Sap," *Phineas and Ferb*. Los Angeles: Walt Disney Television Animation, 2009.

"Just Passing Through," *Phineas and Ferb*. Los Angeles: Walt Disney Television Animation, 2010.

"No More Bunny Business," *Phineas and Ferb*. Los Angeles: Walt Disney Television Animation, 2009.

"Put That Putter Away," *Phineas and Ferb*. Los Angeles: Walt Disney Television Animation, 2008.

"Spa Day," *Phineas and Ferb*. Los Angeles: Walt Disney Television Animation, 2009.

"The Bully Code," *Phineas and Ferb*. Los Angeles: Walt Disney Television Animation, 2009.

Pokemon

"Another One Gabites the Dust," *Pokemon: Diamond and Pearl Galactic Battles*. Tokyo: OLM Inc., 2009.

"Ash Catches a Pokemon," *Pokemon: Indigo League*. Tokyo: OLM Inc., 1998.

"Battling the Generation Gap," *Pokemon: Diamond and Pearl Battle Dimension*. Tokyo: OLM Inc., 2009.

"Challenge of the Samurai," *Pokemon: Indigo League*. Tokyo: OLM Inc., 1998.

"Doc Brock," *Pokemon: Diamond and Pearl Battle Dimension*. Tokyo: OLM Inc., 2009.

"Dueling Heroes," *Pokemon: Master Quest*. Tokyo: OLM Inc., 2002.

"Get the Show on The Road," *Pokemon: Advanced*. Tokyo: OLM Inc., 2003.

"Pokemon Emergency," *Pokemon: Indigo League*. Tokyo: OLM Inc., 1998.

"Pokemon I Choose You," *Pokemon: Indigo League.* Tokyo: OLM Inc., 1998.

"Showdown in Pewter City," *Pokemon: Indigo League.* Tokyo: OLM Inc., 1998.

"Stealing the Conversation," *Pokemon: Diamond and Pearl Galactic Battles.* Tokyo: OLM Inc., 2009.

"The Perfect Match," *Pokemon: Master Quest.* Tokyo: OLM Inc., 2002.

"You Never Can Taillow," *Pokemon: Advanced.* Tokyo: OLM Inc., 2003.

Power Rangers: RPM

"Fade to Black," *Power Rangers: RPM.* North Hollywood, CA: BVS Entertainment, 2009.

"Dr. K," *Power Rangers: RPM.* North Hollywood, CA: BVS Entertainment, 2009.

"Rain," *Power Rangers: RPM.* North Hollywood, CA: BVS Entertainment, 2009.

"Ranger Blue," *Power Rangers: RPM.* North Hollywood, CA: BVS Entertainment, 2009.

"Ranger Green," *Power Rangers: RPM.* North Hollywood, CA: BVS Entertainment, 2009.

"Ranger Red," *Power Rangers: RPM.* North Hollywood, CA: BVS Entertainment, 2009.

"Ranger Yellow Part 1," *Power Rangers: RPM*. North Hollywood, CA: BVS Entertainment, 2009.

"Ranger Yellow Part 2," *Power Rangers: RPM*. North Hollywood, CA: BVS Entertainment, 2009.

"Road to Corinth," *Power Rangers: RPM*. North Hollywood, CA: BVS Entertainment, 2009.

Scooby-Doo, Where Are You?

"A Night of Fright is No Delight," *Scooby-Doo, Where Are You?* Los Angeles: Hanna Barbera, 1970.

"A Tiki Scare is No Fair," *Scooby-Doo, Where Are You?* Los Angeles: Hanna Barbera, 1970.

"Jeepers It's the Creeper," *Scooby-Doo, Where Are You?* Los Angeles: Hanna Barbera, 1970.

"That's Snow Ghost," *Scooby-Doo, Where Are You?* Los Angeles: Hanna Barbera, 1970.

Shaun the Sheep

"Buzz Off Bees," *Shaun the Sheep*. Bristol, UK: Aardman Animations Ltd., 2007.

"Fleeced," *Shaun the Sheep*. Bristol, UK: Aardman Animations Ltd., 2007.

"Mountains Out of Molehills," *Shaun the Sheep*. Bristol, UK: Aardman Animations Ltd., 2007.

"Mower Mouth," *Shaun the Sheep.* Bristol, UK: Aardman Animations Ltd., 2007.

"Off the Baa," *Shaun the Sheep.* Bristol, UK: Aardman Animations Ltd., 2007.

"Shaun Shoots the Sheep," *Shaun the Sheep.* Bristol, UK: Aardman Animations Ltd., 2007.

"Things that Go Bump," *Shaun the Sheep.* Bristol, UK: Aardman Animations Ltd., 2007.

"Timmy in a Tizzy," *Shaun the Sheep.* Bristol, UK: Aardman Animations Ltd., 2007.

Spectacular Spider-Man

"Accomplices," *Spectacular Spider-Man.* Los Angeles: Marvel Animation, 2009.

"Destructive Testing," *Spectacular Spider-Man.* Los Angeles: Marvel Animation, 2009.

"First Steps," *Spectacular Spider-Man.* Los Angeles: Marvel Animation, 2009.

"Gangland," *Spectacular Spider-Man.* Los Angeles: Marvel Animation, 2009.

"Growing Pains," *Spectacular Spider-Man.* Los Angeles: Marvel Animation, 2009.

"Identity Crisis," *Spectacular Spider-Man.* Los Angeles: Marvel Animation, 2009.

"Probable Cause," *Spectacular Spider-Man*. Los Angeles: Marvel Animation, 2009.

"Reinforcement," *Spectacular Spider-Man*. Los Angeles: Marvel Animation, 2009.

"Shear Strength," *Spectacular Spider-Man*. Los Angeles: Marvel Animation, 2009.

"Subtext," *Spectacular Spider-Man*. Los Angeles: Marvel Animation, 2009.

Spider-Man

"The Power of Dr. Octopus," *Spider-Man*. Grantray Lawrence Animation, 1967.

SpongeBob SquarePants

"Enemy-in-Law," *SpongeBob SquarePants*. Los Angeles: United Plankton Pictures, 2005.

"Funny Pants," *SpongeBob SquarePants*. Los Angeles: United Plankton Pictures, 2005.

"Grandma's Kisses," *SpongeBob SquarePants*. Los Angeles: United Plankton Pictures, 2000.

"Karate Island," *SpongeBob SquarePants*. Los Angeles: United Plankton Pictures, 2006.

"Krusty Towers," *SpongeBob SquarePants*. Los Angeles: United Plankton Pictures, 2006.

"Mermaid Man and Barnacle Boy," *SpongeBob SquarePants*. Los Angeles: United Plankton Pictures, 1999.

"Mrs. Puff: You're Fired," *SpongeBob SquarePants*. Los Angeles: United Plankton Pictures, 2006.

"Selling Out," *SpongeBob SquarePants*. Los Angeles: United Plankton Pictures, 2005.

"Squidville," *SpongeBob SquarePants*. Los Angeles: United Plankton Pictures, 2000.

"Whale of a Birthday," *SpongeBob SquarePants*. Los Angeles: United Plankton Pictures, 2006.

Star Wars: The Clone Wars

"Ambush," *Star Wars: The Clone Wars*. San Francisco: Lucasfilm Animation, 2008.

"ARC Troopers," *Star Wars: The Clone Wars*. San Francisco: Lucasfilm Animation, 2010.

"Clone Cadets," *Star Wars: The Clone Wars*. San Francisco: Lucasfilm Animation, 2010.

"Downfall of a Droid," *Star Wars: The Clone Wars*. San Francisco: Lucasfilm Animation, 2008.

"Holocron Heist," *Star Wars: The Clone Wars*. San Francisco: Lucasfilm Animation, 2009.

"Lethal Trackdown," *Star Wars: The Clone Wars*. San Francisco: Lucasfilm Animation, 2010.

"R2 Come Home," *Star Wars: The Clone Wars*. San Francisco: Lucasfilm Animation, 2010.

"Rising Malevolence," *Star Wars: The Clone Wars*. San Francisco: Lucasfilm Animation, 2008.

"Shadow of Malevolence," *Star Wars: The Clone Wars*. San Francisco: Lucasfilm Animation, 2008.

"The Academy," *Star Wars: The Clone Wars*. San Francisco: Lucasfilm Animation, 2010.

Super Friends

"Battle of the Gods," *Super Friends*. Los Angeles: Hanna-Barbera, 1978.

"The Androids," *Super Friends*. Los Angeles: Hanna-Barbera, 1973.

"The Brain Machine," *Super Friends*. Los Angeles: Hanna-Barbera, 1977.

"The Weather Maker," *Super Friends*. Los Angeles: Hanna-Barbera, 1973.

Super Hero Squad

"And Lo…A Pilot Shall Come," *Super Hero Squad*. Los Angeles: Marvel Animation, 2010.

"Deadly is the Black Widow's Bite," *Super Hero Squad*. Los Angeles: Marvel Animation, 2009.

"Night in the Sanctorum," *Super Hero Squad*. Los Angeles: Marvel Animation, 2009.

"This Forest Green," *Super Hero Squad*. Los Angeles: Marvel Animation, 2009.

"This Silver, This Surfer," *Super Hero Squad*. Los Angeles: Marvel Animation, 2009.

"Tremble at the Might of M.O.D.O.K," *Super Hero Squad*. Los Angeles: Marvel Animation, 2009.

"Wrath of the Red Skull," *Super Hero Squad*. Los Angeles: Marvel Animation, 2010.

The Fairly Odd Parents

"Chindred Spirits," *The Fairly Odd Parents*. New York: Frederator Studios, 2008.

"Vicky Gets Fired," *The Fairly Odd Parents*. Los Angeles: Frederator Studios, 2008.

The Scooby-Doo Show

"A Highland Fling with a Monstrous Thing," *Scooby-Doo, Where Are You?* Los Angeles: Hanna Barbera, 1978.

"A Scary Night with a Snow Beast Fright," *Scooby-Doo, Where Are You?* Los Angeles: Hanna Barbera, 1978.

"Make a Beeline Away from That Feline," *Scooby-Doo, Where Are You?* Los Angeles: Hanna Barbera, 1978.

"The Beast is Awake in Bottomless Lake," *Scooby-Doo, Where Are You?* Los Angeles: Hanna Barbera, 1978.

"The Ozark Witch Switch," *Scooby-Doo, Where Are You?* Los Angeles: Hanna Barbera, 1977.

"Watt a Shocking Ghost," *Scooby-Doo, Where Are You?* Los Angeles: Hanna Barbera, 1976.

Time Warp Trio

"Breaking the Codex," *Time Warp Trio.* Boston, MA: WGBH Educational Foundation, 2005.

"The High and the Flighty," *Time Warp Trio.* Boston, MA: WGBH Educational Foundation, 2005.

"The Not-So-Jolly Roger," *Time Warp Trio.* Boston, MA: WGBH Educational Foundation, 2005.

Totally Spies

"Planet of the Hunks," *Totally Spies.* Paris: Marathon Production, 2004.

"Totally Icky," *Totally Spies.* Paris: Marathon Production, 2010.

What's New, Scooby-Doo?

"Scooby-Doo Halloween," *What's New Scooby-Doo.* Burbank, CA: Warner Brothers, 2003.

"A Scooby-Doo Christmas," *What's New Scooby-Doo.* Burbank, CA: Warner Brothers, 2002.

"There's No Creature Like Snow Creature," *What's New Scooby-Doo.* Burbank, CA: Warner Brothers, 2002.

"Space Ape at the Cape," *What's New Scooby-Doo*. Burbank, CA: Warner Brothers, 2002.

Wolverine and the X-Men

"Battle Lines," *Wolverine and the X-Men*. Los Angeles: Marvel Animation, 2009.

"Hindsight, Part 1," *Wolverine and the X-Men*. DVD. Los Angeles: Marvel Animation, 2009.

"Hindsight, Part 2," *Wolverine and the X-Men*. DVD. Los Angeles: Marvel Animation, 2009.

"Hindsight, Part 3," *Wolverine and the X-Men*. DVD. Los Angeles: Marvel Animation, 2009.

"Overflow," *Wolverine and the X-Men*. DVD. Los Angeles: Marvel Animation, 2009.

"Thieves' Gambit," *Wolverine and the X-Men*. DVD. Los Angeles: Marvel Animation, 2009.

"Time Bomb," *Wolverine and the X-Men*. DVD. Los Angeles: Marvel Animation, 2009.

"X-Calibre," *Wolverine and the X-Men*. DVD. Los Angeles: Marvel Animation, 2009.

"Wolverine vs. The Hulk," *Wolverine and the X-Men*. DVD. Los Angeles: Marvel Animation, 2009.

Movies

A Bug's Life. DVD. Directed by John Lasseter and Andrew Stanton. Emeryville, CA: Pixar Animation Studios, 1998.

Barnyard. DVD. Directed by Steve Oedekerk. Hollywood: Paramount Pictures, 2006.

Bee Movie. DVD. Directed by Steve Hickner and Simon J. Smith. Universal City, CA: Dreamworks, 2007.

Cars. DVD. Directed by John Lasseter and Joe Ranft. Emeryville, CA: Pixar Animation Studios, 2006.

Cloudy With a Chance of Meatballs. Directed by Phil Lord and Chris Miller. Culver City, CA: Sony Pictures Animation, 2009.

Everyone's Hero. DVD. Directed by Colin Brady, Christopher Reeve, and Dan St. Pierre. Toronto: Dan Krech Productions, 2006.

Fantastic Mr. Fox. Directed by Wes Anderson. Los Angeles: Twentieth Century Fox Animation Studios, 2009.

Finding Nemo. DVD. Directed by Andrew Stanton and Lee Unkrich. Emeryville, CA: Pixar Animation Studios, 2003.

Happy Feet. DVD. Directed by George Miller, Warren Coleman and Judy Morris. Beverly Hills, CA: Village Roadshow Pictures, 2006.

Ice Age. DVD. Directed by Chris Wedge and Carlos Saldanha. Greenwich, CT: Blue Sky Studios, 2002.

Ice Age 3: Dawn of the Dinosaurs. Directed by Carlos Saldanha and Mike Thurmeier. Greenwich, CT: Blue Sky Studios, 2009.

The Incredibles. DVD. Directed by Brad Bird. Emeryville, CA: Pixar Animation Studios, 2004.

Kiki's Delivery Service. DVD. Directed by Hayao Miyazaki. Koganei-shi: Studio Ghibli, 1989.

Kung Fu Panda. DVD. Directed by Mark Osborne and John Stevenson. Glendale, CA: Dreamworks Animation, 2008.

Monsters, Inc. DVD. Directed by Pete Docter, David Silverman, and Lee Unkrich. Emeryville, CA: Pixar Animation Studios, 2001.

Monsters vs. Aliens. DVD. Directed by Rob Letterman and Conrad Vernon. Universal City, CA: Dreamworks, 2009.

Mulan. DVD. Directed by Tony Bancroft and Barry Cook. Burbank, CA:Walt Disney Feature Animation, 1998.

Ponyo. Directed by Hayao Miyazaki. Koganei-shi: Studio Ghibli, 2009.

Ratatouille. DVD. Directed by Brad Bird and Jan Pinkava. Emeryville, CA: Pixar Animation Studios, 2007.

Shrek the Third. DVD. Directed by Chris Miller and Raman Hui. Universal City, CA: Dreamworks, 2007.

Star Wars: Episode I – The Phantom Menace. Directed by George Lucas. San Francisco: Lucasfilm, 1999.

Star Wars: Episode II – Attack of the Clones. Directed by George Lucas. San Francisco: Lucasfilm, 2002.

Star Wars: The Clone Wars. DVD. Directed by Dave Filoni. San Francisco: Lucasfilm, 2008.

The Tale of Despereaux. DVD. Directed by Steven Fell and Robert Stevenhagen. Universal City, CA: Universal Pictures, 2008.

Toy Story. DVD. Directed by John Lasseter. Emeryville, CA: Pixar Animation Studios, 1995.

Toy Story 2. DVD. Directed by John Lasseter, Ash Brannon and Lee Unkrich. Emeryville, CA: Pixar Animation Studios, 1999.

Toy Story 3. Directed by Lee Unkrich. Emeryville, CA: Pixar Animation Studios, 2010.

Wall-E. DVD. Directed by Andrew Stanton. Emeryville, CA: Pixar Animation Studios, 2008.

Wallace & Gromit in Three Amazing Adventures. DVD. Directed by Nick Park. Bristol, UK: Aardman, 2006.

Video Games

Mario & Luigi: Bowser's Inside Story. Kyoto: Nintendo, 2009.

Mario & Sonic at the Olympic Summer Games. San Francisco: Sega of America, 2007.

Mario & Sonic at the Olympic Winter Games. San Francisco: Sega of America. 2009.

Mario Kart. Kyoto: Nintendo, 2008.

MySims: Agents. Redwood City, CA: Electronic Arts, 2009.

New Super Mario Brothers. Kyoto: Nintendo, 2009.

Index

movies
  recommended 164
Mudshark 81, 158
Mulan 49
Munsch, Robert 47, 66, 81, 139, 151
muscularity 96, 100
MySims Agents 120, 164

N

Nate the Great 158
Nathanson, Paul 23
nerd 31, 98
  as insult 2, 116
  as stereotype 14, 31, 67, 98, 131
  in warrior discourse 14
Ni Hao Kai-Lan 5

O

objectification, female 89
Olivia 5
omega
  in male hierarchy 22
Oppel, Kenneth 157
Osborne, Mary Pope 157
Owens, R. Glynn 97

P

Paper Bag Princess, The 47, 139
Parker, Peter 30, 67, 97, 98, 102, 119
Patroclus 13
Paulsen, Gary 158
Penguins of Madagascar 77
Phineas and Ferb 32, 55, 77, 116
  Candace 39, 112, 113, 118
  Doofenshmirtz 116, 117
  Isabella 39, 111
picture books
  portrayal of fathers 46, 67
  portrayal of mothers 46, 66
  recommended 153
Pigtail Pals 146

Pilkey, Dav 114
Pippi Longstocking 155
Pokemon 27, 49, 62, 78
  Ash 61
  Brock 60, 133
  female characters 37, 112, 118
Pollack, William 32, 84
Ponyo 60
Pope, Harrison 148
Power Rangers RPM 27, 29, 60, 114
  Dillon 24
  Dr. K 79
  Scott 24, 49
  Summer 79
  Ziggy 33, 113
Psychology of men's health, The 97

Q

Quinn, Suzanne Flannery 46, 47

R

Radical Parenting 126
Raising Cain 101, 147
Rashbaum, Beth 11, 57, 63, 66, 148
Ratatouille 71
  Colette 74
  Remy 52, 60, 62
Real Boys 32
Reeves, Steve 99
Rey, Margaret and H.A. 151, 152, 178
Reynolds, Peter H. 152
role model, male 129, 156, 157, 158

S

Salamander Room, The 151
Scaredy Squirrel 153
Scarry, Richard 152
Scieszka, Jon 82
Scooby-Doo 33, 113
Scooby-Doo Show, The 79, 160
Scooby-Doo, Where Are You? 79, 160

Endnotes

—————

Introduction

[1] Levant, Ronald F. "Men and Masculinity," in Vol. 2 of *Encyclopedia of Women and Gender: Sex Similarities and Differences and the Impact of Society on Gender.* ed. Judith Worrell. (San Diego: Academic Press, 2001), 717-727. Levant has written extensively on family and gender psychology. His full bio is available at http://www.drronaldlevant.com/bio.html.

[2] Lee, Christina and R. Glynn Owens. *The psychology of men's health.* (Buckingham: Open University Press, 2002), 73-76.

[3] Brescoll, Victoria L. and Eric Luis Uhlmann. "Attitudes Toward Traditional and Nontraditional Parents." *Psychology of Women Quarterly* 29, no. 4 (2005): 436-445.

[4] Lee and Owens, p. 73-79.

[5] Silverstein, Olga and Beth Rashbaum. *The Courage to Raise Good Men.* (New York: Penguin Books, 1994), 9.

[6] *Achilles,* http://en.wikipedia.org/wiki/Achilles#Birth, Accessed on March 28, 2010.

[7] Statius, Publius Papinius. *The Achilleid* 2. 94-159.

[8] Statius, 1.

[9] Statius, 2. 23 – 42.

[10] Homer, Books 19 and 20.

217

11 Jordan, Ellen. (1995) "Fighting Boys and Fantasy Play: the construction of masculinity in the early years of school." *Gender and Education* 7, no. 1, (1995): 69 – 86.

12 Nathanson, Paul and Katherine K. Young. *Spreading Misandry: The Teaching of Contempt for Men in Popular Culture.* (Montréal: McGill-Queen's University Press, 2001), 8.

13 Ryan, Erin. "Dora the Explorer: Giving Power to Preschoolers, Girls, and Latinas" (Paper presented at the annual meeting of the Association for Education in Journalism and Mass Communication, The Renaissance, Washington, DC, August 8, 2007.) http://www.allacademic.com/meta/p203514_index.html.

14 Sun, Chyng. *Mickey Mouse Monopoly: Disney, Childhood & Corporate Power.* Transcript. (Northampton, MA: Media Education Foundation, 2001), 5.

15 Ward, L. Monique and Allison Caruthers. "Media Influences," in Vol. 2 of *Encyclopedia of Women and Gender: Sex Similarities and Differences and the Impact of Society on Gender.* ed. Judith Worrell. (San Diego: Academic Press, 2001), 696.

Chapter 1

1 Note that I have chosen to use terms like *wimp, nerd* and *geek* not to condone that attitude towards "weak" boys or show support for use of that word, but to define and discuss the stereotype that is so prevalent in our society.

2 Nathanson and Young. *Spreading Misandry,* 81.

3 Teletoon Bakugan Battle Brawlers page, accessed October 3, 2009, http://www.teletoon.com/teletoon3/teletoon.php?language=En&func=php|templates/show.php|../tv/bakugan/bakugan_en.xml&xVar= .

4 Ibid.

5 Dorling Kindersely Ltd. *Star Wars: The Clone Wars Character Encyclopedia.* (New York: Dorling Kindersley, 2010), 164.

[6] Hobbes, Nicholas. *Essential Militaria.* (Toronto: McArthur & Company, 2004), 14.

[7] Machiavelli, Niccolo. *The Art of War.* 1521. Translated by Neal Wood. (Cambridge, MA: Da Capo Press, 2001), xxxii, lxxvii.

[8] Dunnigan, James F. *How to Make War: A Comprehensive Guide to Modern Warfare in the Twenty-First Century,* 4th ed. (New York: HarperCollins,Quill, 2003), 288-290.

[9] National Research Council. *Human Behaviour in Military Contexts.* Edited by James J. Blascovich and Christine R. Hartel. (Washington, DC: The National Academies Press, 2008), 55-57.

[10] "Army Master Resilience Training course provides valued instruction," accessed August 15, 2010, "http://www.army.mil/-news/2010/03/29/36520-army-master-resilience-training-course-provides-valued-instruction/.

[11] Lego Skrall character description, accessed August 15, 2010, http://bionicle.lego.com/en-us/story/bios/glatorian/Skrall.aspx.

[12] Jordan, Ellen. "Fighting Boys and Fantasy Play, 69 – 86.

[13] Ibid, 76.

[14] "Starting Line," *Hot Wheels Battle Force 5.* Toronto: Nelvana, 2009.

[15] Cowell, Cressida. *How to Train Your Dragon.* London: Hachette Children's Books, 2003, 24.

[16] Ibid, 11, 123.

[17] Pollack, William. *Real Boys: Rescuing Our Sons from the Myths of Boyhood.* (New York: Random House, 1998), 24.

[18] Pilkey, Dav. *Captain Underpants and the Invasion of the Incredibly Naughty Cafeteria Ladies from Outer Space (and the Subsequent Assault of the Equally Evil Lunchroom Zombie Nerds).* (New York: Scholastic Inc., 1999), 15.

[19] Pilkey, Dav. *Captain Underpants and the Perilous Plot of Professor Poopypants.* (New York: Scholastic Inc., 2001), 17-19.

[20] Pilkey, Dav. *Captain Underpants and the Wrath of the Wicked Wedgie Woman.* (New York: Scholastic Inc., 2000), 15.

21 Hamilton, "Gender stereotyping and under-representation of female characters in 200 popular children's picture books."

22 Wood, Eileen, Serge Desmarais and Sara Gugula. "The impact of parenting experience on gender stereotyped toy play of children." *Sex Roles* 47, no. 1-2 (2002): 39-49.

23 Sun, Chyng. *Mickey Mouse Monopoly: Disney, Childhood & Corporate Power.* Transcript. (Northampton, MA: Media Education Foundation, 2001), 5.

24 "Enemy-in-Law," *SpongeBob SquarePants*, Nickelodeon, 2005.

25 "And Lo...A Pilot Shall Come," *Super Hero Squad*. Los Angeles: Marvel Animation, 2010.

26 Witt, Susan D. (1997). "Parental influence on children's socialization to gender roles." *Adolescence.* 32, no. 126 (1997): 253-260.

Chapter 2

1 Sacks, Glenn and Richard Samglick. "Advertisers: Men Are Not Idiots." *Advertising Age*, April 14, 2008.

2 "TV Dads: Backgrounder for Teachers," Media Awareness Network, accessed May 24, 2009, http://www.media-awareness.ca/english/resources/educational/teaching_backgrounders/stereotyping/tv_dads_backgrounder.cfm.

3 "Mother's Day ...by the numbers," Statistics Canada, accessed May 29, 2010, http://www42.statcan.ca/smr08/2006/smr08_047_2006-eng.htm.

4 U.S. Census Bureau. "Facts for Features: Unmarried and Single Americans Week Sept. 20-26, 2009." *U.S. Census Bureau News*, July 21, 2009.

5 Miss Corolle product page, accessed April 27, 2010, http://www.corolle.com/us/catalogue/misscorolle.php5#intro.

6 Wood, Eileen, Serge Desmarais and Sara Gugula. "The impact of parenting experience on gender stereotyped toy play of children." *Sex Roles* 47, no. 1-2 (2002): 39-49.

[7] Pike, Jennifer and Nancy A. Jennings. "The effects of commercials on children's perception of gender appropriate toy use." *Sex Roles* 52, no. 1-2 (2005): 83-91.

[8] Anderson, David A. and Mykol Hamilton "Gender role stereotyping of parents in children's picture books: the invisible father." *Sex Roles* 52, no. 3-4 (2005): 145-151.

[9] Quinn, Susan M. Flannery. "The depictions of fathers and children in best-selling picture books in the United States: a hybrid semiotic analysis." *Fathering.* March 22, 2009.

Chapter 3

[1] Silverstein and Rashbaum, 5, 9, 11, 13.

[2] Ibid.

[3] Statius, Publius Papinius. *The Achilleid*, (Cambridge, MA: Harvard University Press, 2003), accessed March 28, 2010, http://www.theoi.com/Text/StatiusAchilleid1A.html.

[4] Holland, Jack. *Misogyny: The World's Oldest Prejudice.* (New York: Carroll & Graf Publishers, 2006), 13-14.

[5] *Star Wars: Episode II – Attack of the Clones.* Directed by George Lucas. San Francisco: Lucasfilm, 2002.

[6] Götz, Maya et al. *Girls and Boys and Television: A few reminders for more gender sensitivity in children's TV.* Munich: International Central Institute for Youth and Educational Television, 2008.

[7] Blakemore, Judith E. Owen and Renee E. Centers. "Characteristics of boys' and girls' toys." *Sex Roles* 53, no. 9-10 (2005): 619-633.

[8] Boys' Role Play page on Toys R Us site, accessed May 23, 2010. http://www.toysrus.ca/category/index.jsp?categoryId=4192048&cp=4192048&clickid=leftnav_cat_txt, Girls' Role Play page on Toys R Us site, accessed March 23, 2010. http://www.toysrus.ca/category/index.jsp?categoryId=4192046&cp=4192046&clickid=leftnav_cat_txt.

[9] Boys' Make Believe page on Chapters/Indigo site, accessed July 11, 2010. http://www.chapters.indigo.ca/toys/Boys/606324-750072-

750074-700014-606329-cat.html, Girls' Make Believe page on Chapters/Indigo Site, accessed July 11, 2010, http://www.chapters.indigo.ca/toys/Girls/606324-750072-750074-700014-606330-cat.html.

10 Hamilton, "Gender stereotyping and under-representation of female characters in 200 popular children's picture books."

Chapter 4

1 Hamilton, "Gender stereotyping and under-representation of female characters in 200 popular children's picture books", 757.

2 Götz, Maya et al. *Girls and Boys and Television: A few reminders for more gender sensitivity in children's TV*, 2.

3 Ibid.

4 Smith, Dr. Stacy L. and Cooke, Crystal Allene. *Gender Stereotypes: An Analysis of Popular Films and TV.* (Los Angeles: Geena Davis Institute on Gender in Media, 2008), 12-13.

5 Oleck, Joan. (2006). "Gender Stereotypes Still Persist in Films." *School Library Journal*, November 3, 2006. http://www.schoollibraryjournal.com/article/CA6387189.html.

6 Dorling Kindersely Ltd. *Star Wars: The Clone Wars Character Encyclopedia.* (New York: Dorling Kindersley, 2010).

7 "Totally Icky", *Totally Spies.* Paris: Marathon Production, 2010.

8 "Agents of Success," Accessed October 16, 2010, http://goliath.ecnext.com/coms2/gi_0199-6892323/Agents-of-success-while-it.html

9 "Wrath of the Red Skull," *Super Hero Squad.* Los Angeles: Marvel Animation, 2010.

10 "And Lo…A Pilot Shall Come," *Super Hero Squad.* Los Angeles: Marvel Animation, 2010.

11 Girls' Role Play page on Toys R Us site, accessed August 29, 2010. http://www.toysrus.ca/category/index.jsp?categoryId=4192046&cp=4192046&clickid=leftnav_cat_txt.

[12] Kids 5-8, Girls on Chapters/Indigo site, accessed December 15, 2009. http://www.chapters.indigo.ca/toys/Girls/606324-750072-750074-606335-606330-cat.html.

[13] "Books That Guys Read," Guys Read, accessed August 2009. http://www.guysread.com/books/.

[14] McDonald, Megan. *Judy Moody*. (Somerville. Candlewick Press, 2000), 23.

[15] Pollack, William. *Real Boys: Rescuing Our Sons from the Myths of Boyhood*. (New York: Random House, 1998), 24.

Chapter 5

[1] Daniels, Les. *Superman: The Complete History*. (San Francisco: Chronicle Books, 1998), 31.

[2] Jordan, Ellen. "Fighting Boys and Fantasy Play", 69 – 86.

[3] Holland, Penny. *We don't play with guns here: War, weapon and superhero play in the early years*. (Berkshire: Open University Press, 2003), 100.

[4] "Night in the Sanctorum," *Super Hero Squad*. Los Angeles: Marvel Animation, 2009.

[5] Children Now. *Boys to Men: Media Messages About Masculinity*. Oakland: Children Now, 2000, 11.

[6] UFC Action Figure Karo Parysian page on Toys R Us site, accessed August 28, 2010, http://www.toysrus.ca/product/index.jsp?productId=4277397&prodFindSrc=search.

[7] "On-Air Personalities" *MLB.com,* accessed on August 28, 2010. http://mlb.mlb.com/network/personalities/.

[8] Hardin, Marie and Jennifer D. Greer. "The influence of gender-role socialization, media use and sports participation on perceptions of gender-appropriate sports." *Journal of Sports Behavior* 32 (June 1, 2009).

[9] Women's Sports Foundation, "Women Play Sports but Not on TV," *Women's Sports Foundation,* June 4, 2010, accessed on August 28, 2010.

http://womenssportsfoundation.org/Content/Articles/Research/W/Women-play-sports-but-not-on-TV.aspx.

10 Messner, Michael, "Dropping the Ball on Covering Women's Sports, *The Huffington Post*, June 3, 2010, accessed August 28, 2010. http://www.huffingtonpost.com/michael-messner/dropping-the-ball-on-cove_b_599912.html.

11 Perkins, Dave. "Milquetoast Blue Jays could use a little moxie." *The Toronto Star*. August 21, 2009.

12 Canadian Sports Hall of Fame, Honoured Members—Doug Flutie, accessed on August 28, 2010, http://cshof.ca/accessible/hm_profile.php?i=489.

13 Pompei, Dan. "Corner McMillian thrives despite lack of ideal size" in *The Sporting News*, November 16, 1998, accessed on August 28, 2010 on http://findarticles.com/p/articles/mi_m1208/is_1998_Nov_16/ai_53256082/.

14 Cohn, Bob. "Clarion's Hoggard piques NFL interest despite his size," Pittsburgh Tribune-Review, August 22, 2010, accessed August 28, 2010, http://www.pittsburghlive.com/x/pittsburghtrib/sports/college/s_695947.html.

15 Yessie, Ryan. "Ryan Yessie's Top 50 for 2010: Part 2 – 11 to 30", *OHL Prospects* (blog), May 31, 2010, accessed August 28, 2010, http://ohlprospects.blogspot.com/2010/05/ryan-yessies-top-50-for-2010-part-2-11.html.

16 Laskaris, Sam, "Amestoy Reaches Great Heights Despite Small Stature", *Hockey Now, Ontario Edition*, accessed August 28, 2010, http://www.ontariohockey.com/story/25/Junior%20A%20Report/4958/Amestoy_Reaches_Great_Heights_Despite_Small_Stature.aspx.

17 Messner, Mike et al. *Boys to Men: Sports Media Messages About Masculinity.* Oakland: Children Now, 1999, 3-4.

18 Hall, Joseph. "Young children feel the weight of body image." *The Toronto Star*. August 27, 2009.

19 Pope, Harrison et al. *The Adonis Complex.* (New York: Touchstone, 2000), 28, 174.

[20] Common Sense Media, "Boys and Body Image Tips", *Common Sense Media*, accessed August 27, 2009, http://www.commonsensemedia.org/boys-and-body-image-tips.

[21] Smolak, Linda "Body Image Development in Children" in *Body Image: A Handbook of Theory, Research, and Clinical Practice.*, 66-68.

[22] Lee, Christina and R. Glynn Owens. *The psychology of men's health.* (Buckingham: Open University Press, 2002), 57.

[23] Spettigue, Wendy and Katherine A. Henderson. "Eating Disorders and the Role of the Media", *The Canadian Child and Adolescent Psychiatry Review*, 13, no. 1 (2004): 16-19.

[24] Tiggeman, Marika. "Media Influences on Body Image Development" in *Body Image: A Handbook of Theory, Research, and Clinical Practice.* (New York: The Guilford Press, 2002), 96.

[25] Corson, Patricia Westmoreland and Arnold E. Andersen. "Body Image Issues Among Boys and Men" in *Body Image: A Handbook of Theory, Research, and Clinical Practice*, 193.

[26] Barlett, Chris et al. Action Figures and Men. Sex Roles. December 2005.

[27] Christina Lee is Professor and Director of the Research Centre for Gender and Health at the University of Newcastle, Australia. Glynn Owens is Professor of Health Psychology at the University of Auckland, New Zealand. (http://www.mcgraw-hill.co.uk/html/0335207057.html)

[28] Lee, Christina and R. Glynn Owens. *The psychology of men's health.* (Buckingham: Open University Press, 2002), 57, 68.

[29] Smith and Cook, *Gender Stereotypes: An Analysis of Popular Films and TV*, 12-17.

[30] "Man and Iron Man," *Iron Man: Armored Adventures*, Marvel Animation, 2009.

[31] Pope et al, 34.

[32] Etcoff, Nancy. *Survival of the Prettiest.* (New York: Doubleday, 1999), 179.

[33] Pope, Harrison et al, 41-42.

[34] Pope et al, 43.

35 Biography of Steve Reeves, accessed March 14, 2010, http://www.stevereeves.com/bio-bodybuilder.asp.

36 "Hulk Hogan, on Witness Stand, Tells of Steroid Use in Wrestling," *New York Times Archives*, July 15, 1994, http://www.nytimes.com/1994/07/15/nyregion/hulk-hogan-on-witness-stand-tells-of-steroid-use-in-wrestling.html

37 Hulk Hogan biography, *HulkHogan.net*, accessed October 17, 2010, http://hulkhogan.net/hulk-hogan-biography/hulk-hogan-personal-biography?view=item.

38 Durham, *The Lolita Effect*, 96.

39 Pope et al, 46, 179, 193-194.

40 Lee and Owens, 19-21.

41 Kindlon and Thompson, 143-149.

42 "Hindsight, Part 2," *Wolverine and the X-Men*. DVD. Los Angeles: Marvel Animation, 2009.

43 Hall, Jason. *Justice League: The Animated Series Guide.* (New York: DK Publishing, 2004), 10.

44 Götz, Maya et al. *Girls and Boys and Television*, 11.

Chapter 6

1 Swann, 14-20, 113.

2 Swann, 14-20.

3 Jule, Allyson. *A Beginner's Guide to Language and Gender.* Cleveden: Multilingual Matters, 2008, 83.

4 Swann, 21-23.

5 Smith and Cook, p. 12.

6 Swann, 26-27.

7 "Bakugan Battle Brawlers Cast and Crew", accessed March 16, 2010, http://www.tv.com/bakugan-battle-brawlers/show/75192/cast.html.

8 Swann, 24, 32.

9 Pilkey, Dav. *Captain Underpants and the Perilous Plot of Professor Poopypants*. New York: Scholastic Inc., 2000.

[10] Dav's Books, accessed March 16, 2010, http://www.pilkey.com/bookview.php?id=19.

[11] Bolger, Kevin. *Sir Fartsalot Hunts the Booger*. New York: Penguin, 2008.

[12] Scieszka, Jon. *Knights of the Kitchen Table*. New York: Puffin Books, 1991, 33.

[13] Scieszka, Jon. *Tut Tut*. New York: Puffin Books, 1996, 14, 26, 48.

[14] Stilton, Geronimo. *The Kingdom of Fantasy*. (Toronto: Scholastic Canada Inc., 2009). 140.

[15] Swann, p. 16.

[16] Nelvana Limited. *A Fish Called Tayghen*. Bakugan Battle Brawlers, 2008.

[17] Nelvana Limited. *Dan's Last Stand*. Bakugan Battle Brawlers, 2008.

[18] Scieszka, Jon. *DaWild, DaCrazy, DaVinci*. New York: Puffin Books, 2004, 14, 20, 25.

[19] Various Artists. *SpongeBob's Greatest Hits*. Viacom International Ltd., 2009.

[20] Various Artists. *Phineas and Ferb: Songs From the Hit Disney TV Series*. Walt Disney Records, 2009.

[21] Messner et al, 4.

[22] Red Adventure cape page, accessed March 16, 2010 http://www.chapters.indigo.ca/toys/Red-Adventure-Cape-Small-Great/771877542732-item.html, Purple Princess Cape, accessed March 16, 2010 http://www.chapters.indigo.ca/toys/Purple-Princess-Cape-Medium-Great/771877501456-item.html.

[23] Swann, 46-47.

[24] Warner Brothers Animation. *Scooby Doo Halloween*. What's New Scooby-Doo, 2003.

[25] Teletoon, *What's New Scooby-Doo* page, accessed March 16, 2010, http://www.teletoon.com/teletoon3/teletoon.php?language=En&func=php|templates/show.php|../tv/whatsNewScoobyDoo/whatsNewScoobyDoo_en.xml&xVar=0

26 Columbia Pictures. *Cloudy with a Chance of Meatballs* page, accessed March 16, 2010, http://www.cloudywithachanceofmeatballs.com/.

27 Pixar Films, *Cars* character description pages, accessed March 16, 2010, http://www.pixar.com/featurefilms/cars/characters.html.

28 Teletoon, *Iron Man: Armored Adventures* page, accessed March 16, 2010, http://www.teletoon.com/teletoon3/teletoon.php?language=En&func=php|templates/show.php|../tv/ironManArmoredAdventures/ironManArmoredAdventures_en.xml&xVar=0.

29 Jule, 14.

30 Swann, 36-37.

31 West, Tracey. *The Party Crashers*. New York: Scholastic, 2009, 51.

32 Stilton, *The Kingdom of Fantasy*, i.

33 Sun, Chyng. *Mickey Mouse Monopoly: Disney, Childhood & Corporate Power*. Transcript. (Northampton, MA: Media Education Foundation, 2001), 5.

34 "Rita Mae Brown Quotes", *Brainy Quotes*, Accessed August 28, 2010, http://www.brainyquote.com/quotes/authors/r/rita_mae_brown_2.html

Chapter 7

1 Ormsby, Mary and Leslie Scrivener. "What a 9-Year-Old Thinks." *Toronto Star*, January 31, 2010.

2 Ven Petten, Vanessa. "How to Win the Gender War: Sexism and Teens." *Radical Parenting*, May, 2009. http://www.radicalparenting.com/2009/05/12/how-to-win-the-gender-war-sexism-and-teens-teen-article/.

3 Fine, Cordelia. *Delusions of Gender*. (New York: W.W. Norton & Company, 2010), 200-213.

4 Nerf N-Strike page, Hasbro Toys, accessed February 15, 2010, http://www.hasbro.com/nerf/n-strike/shop/details.cfm?guid=940BFD86-6D40-1014-8BF0-9EFBF894F9D4&product_id=22378.

CPSIA information can be obtained at www.ICGtesting.com
Printed in the USA
BVOW040526021111

275092BV00003B/19/P